The History
of Carver High School
1890 – 1970

ISBN: 978-1-7332503-3-7

Nonfiction
1. History, Interviews, Archival Records 2. Gulf Coast High Schools, Colored Schools, Negro Schools 3. Alumni Association, Scholarships, Students 4. Civic Organization, Community support activities 5. Pascagoula

Published by:
PN/CHS Alumni Association, Inc.
P. O. Box 1761
Pascagoula, MS 39568-1761

Book Cover and Interior Design: Creative Publishing Book Design

The History
of Carver High School
1890 – 1970

FROM THE COLORED SCHOOL
TO
CARVER HIGH SCHOOL

Home
of the
Hornets

**Excerpts From Records and Interviews of the Pascagoula
Negro/Carver High School Alumni Association, Inc.**

Acknowledgments

Editorial Contributor: Attorney Brenda Miller Johnson, the First Wall of Fame Committee Chairperson, Class of 1968, gave valuable feedback on the direction and content of the overall history of Carver High School.

List of Contributors

1. Mr. Joe Davis, PN/CHSAA Heir: provided a photograph of the 1952 Carver High School building plaque.

2. Mrs. Dorothy Richardson Harvey, Class of 1963, provided numerous historical records of the PN/CHSAA, Inc., made phone calls and gave advice which helped to complete this book.

3. Reverend Dr. Ann Tyrus Pickett-Parker, Class of 1960: Researched the writers of current lyrics and music for Carver High School's Alma Mater.

4. Mrs. V. P. Williams-Watts (science and mathematics teacher) directed Robert Jennings, Cecil Paris, and Glenn Larkins—to save numerous documents and school artifacts during the summer of 1970.

5. Mr. Andrew J. Elly, Class of 1967, (1) originated the framework of ideas that lead to the development of the PN/CHS Alumni Association, Inc., along with Dorothy R. Harvey and Dinah Dorsett-Riley; and (2) discussed the Carver High School History Book Project (June 18, 2022) with Dr. Larry G. Hanshaw and requested that he accept the role of Project Coordinator/Editor-Writer with assistance from members of the PN/CHS Archives Committee and others at his discretion.

6. Mr. Michael A. Hanshaw, Class of 1970 and Wall of Fame Committee Chairman, provided dictation software recommendations and technical guidance which saved a ton of time in the preparation of this book.

7. Mr. Jerry Blake, Class of 1957, for the numerous photographs of classmates, friends, and relatives.

8. Mr. J. B. Carter, Class of 1956, for helping our history book project obtain the story of his uncle, Mr. Willie James Smith, age 103. Mr. Carter also provided valuable insights and details about sports, school life, and the civic environment in Pascagoula and Carver High School.

9. Mr. Robert Jennings for his preservation of school artifacts, his many conversations about events germane to this book, and his years of dedicated service as the Archives Committee Chairman.

10. Mrs. Barbara E. Hanshaw for photographs of *Dear Ole Carver High* and the Panther-Gator Challenge game.

11. The PN/CHSAA, Inc. recognizes and thanks:

(a) The Superintendent (Dr. Billy Ellzey) and the Pascagoula Board of Education for their support of the mission of the PN/CHSAA, Inc. We especially applaud their decision to place our Carver High School Hornet on the renovated gymnasium floor that is part of the Aaron Jones Family Interactive Center; (b) Dr. Caterria B. Payton (Principal, Pascagoula High School) for honoring the Hornets of Carver High School during *Black History Month* with a *commemorative t-shirt* (see Appendix 3, Item 4) showing the CHS Hornet, PHS Panther, and the Gautier Gator. The inaugural basketball game (*Panther-Gator Challenge*) and dinner also were thoughtful components of the well-attended program all of which further bonded the relationship between our schools in the Pascagoula-Gautier communities. All activities were elements of the *Black History Month* theme "**Honoring the *Ones Who Paved the Way*";** (c) The Mississippi Press, WLOX Television Station, and all local businesses, donors, and individuals for news coverage and/or purchased advertisements which over the years enabled the success of the civic mission of the PN/CHSAA, Inc.; and (d) The cities of Pascagoula and Gautier, and especially the Pascagoula Police Department, for their past and ongoing support which has enabled nearly 40 years of safe Reunion Balls, Christmas parties, and parade events.

12. Mr. Stanley Moore for accumulating the initial number of PN/CHSAA and Carver High School documents that began efforts to maintain our historical records.

13. Committee Member Pat Davis and the Smithsonian Institution for permitting PN/CHSAA, Inc. use of 13 photographs of panelists and attendees at the 9-27-2022 Smithsonian Voting Rights Exhibit, Performing Arts Center, Pascagoula, MS.

Table of Contents

Foreword

The writing of the history of Carver High School, Pascagoula, Mississippi, is a story that was in the making several years before June 18th, 2022. Discussions about our school's history, for example, have probably been in the minds of its graduates but only a few pages of the school's history found their way into program pamphlets of activities sponsored by the Pascagoula Negro/Carver High School Alumni Association, Inc. (PN/CHSAA). This book will attempt to greatly expand what is known about Carver High by capturing the collective memories and experiences of living alumni in the form of interviews conducted by phone and in person.

Needless to say, we made a conscious decision to gather as much information as possible to promptly and properly prepare the history of our school. For example, several interviews involved people who are currently between 90-103 years old. Others are in their 80s and still others, like me, are in their mid-70s. Other alumni are in their late 60s. Such age groups offered a treasure trove of valuable perspectives about life and the times in which they lived. All of their experiences are grounded in the times when many of our fore-parents could not obtain 12 years of schooling at Carver High. Instead, many left to get the remaining two years in other places in the state of Mississippi or left the state to earn four years of traditional high school education.

These circumstances and many others will be at the heart of our association's efforts to let our living alumni tell their individual stories through interviews. Collectively, therefore, it will be the experiences of alumni that will paint a portrait of what it was like to attend Pascagoula Negro High School and Carver High School while preparing for the challenges we all faced. This seems no different from current students who work hard today in hopes of using their education to make a better life for themselves and their posterity. The history of Carver High School 1890-1970 will not only be our school's history up to the present time but also will be a collection of invaluable stories that will be salient reminders of how far we have come. Moreover, this book will underscore what is currently being done to ensure that Hornets who follow us will receive from us the same support and spirit to succeed given to us by those who came before us. What is the lesson to be learned from our high school's history?

To paraphrase an idea from George Orwell's Animal Farm, it must be our mission to make certain that no person's opportunity in today's America will be crippled by any ideas grounded in beliefs that all Americans are equal but that *some are more equal than others*. Therefore, our heirs must seek to achieve more than their predecessors for no other reason than to remember that people *who do not know their history will be bound to repeat it*. We must look out for each other. I feel certain all Hornets and

Panthers will answer the warning of Frederick Douglas by letting our life achievements be examples for everyone else. A lesson and more from the History of Carver High School.

Larry G. Hanshaw, Ph.D., Project Coordinator/Editor-Writer and Professor Emeritus of Secondary Science Education, The University of Mississippi, Oxford, Mississippi.

Prelude

I magine the awesome task of trying to write a history book. Should it focus only on dates and years or the names of classmates and friends we knew and still have? Or should we remember our history in a broader context beyond buildings constructed and new books we should have received but did not? Not to mention the needless destruction of treasured artifacts as the decade of the 70s had barely started. Then there are the memories of favorite teachers and principals who made us toe the line in tandem with the ever-present voices of parents who provided essential home training; especially as we may have contemplated decisions with unpredictable outcomes.

This history book contains those moments and more. Rather than pick and choose which elements shaped our lives as Hornets more than others, we accept that all of these bits of memories, including, of course, the presence of the Almighty. Likewise, we remember our school days and the many positive messages of songs and the artists who performed them. Some of the advice is timeless. For example, in our Alma Mater, we proudly sing now as we did then "Dear Carver High, we love thee" and in another moment, we reflect on the timeless advice teachers and parents often gave us.

Today, some of that advice is captured in the words of B.B. King's *Better Not Look Back*. The idea of "*keeping the hammer down*" comes to mind whenever things do not turn out as planned. Perhaps you feel the same way. Our African American roots are filled with a touch of this and a touch of that to help us make it through the day. For example, our beloved librarian, Mrs. Jennings, typifies the many "givers of wisdom" who guided our years at school. She often said to those of us who stared at the clock on the wall and loudly closed our books much too early before the bell sounded: "all of you clock-watchers should consider that time will pass, will you?" I remember that as though it was yesterday. Never be in a hurry to shut down the opportunity to learn as much as you can. Thanks, Mrs. Jennings.

I can also share that on some days, especially upon reflection of friends and classmates who are with us in spirit only, I think of the lessons learned playing in the band as well as lessons learned singing in the choir at school and church. I know I am not the only one. The voice training at school and church were inseparable. Even now I find myself in a good spiritual place when I put those sources of training to work when I sing a favorite song "I Won't Complain". You probably have a favorite song or more as well. Having been a student at Carver High, gave me a voice for songs whether in the church or the shower. I am certain I am not alone when I think of Mr. Marvin Pickett and Mr. Richard Moore, who helped us sing better than we ever thought possible. Your story may be similar to mine for different reasons and may involve other teachers and leaders at Dear Ole Carver High.

As you read this book, other Hornets will share many memories of amazing stories of how they got to where they are today. I believe you may laugh and perhaps cry as you read The History of Carver High School: 1890 – 1970 (and beyond). Enjoy.

Mrs. Mattie Woods Jennings, PNHS/CHS Librarian and teacher.

Overview

A: Scope and Description of the Carver High School History Project

During a conversation in June of 2022 with Andrew J. Elly, President of the PN/CHS Alumni Association, Inc., Class of 1967, the writing of the History of Carver High School came up. The wide-ranging discussion touched on many aspects of what the Association has done over the years. Eventually, President Elly asked me if I would consider spearheading an effort to write our school's history. Given our ages and ages of those older and younger than either of us, I consented to lend my support to make this book project become a reality. Several phone calls later, I was immersed in historical documents given to me by Dorothy Richardson Harvey, another long-serving officer of the PN/CHSAA. She handed me a large bag filled with documents and wished me success! It became obvious from later discussions about the historical record with Robert Jennings (Archives Committee Chairperson, Class of 1960) and J.B. Carter, Class of 1956, that we should get started as soon as possible. The impetus was clear: two alumni were past the age of 95, one age 91, and another age 103. Subsequently, using regular alumni meetings, Facebook, word of mouth, phone calls, and emails, the history book effort circulated. In less than three weeks, a large 3-ring binder was nearing its capacity covering four areas: (1) the history of our school; (2) an interview component derived from five questions to which alumni responded, (3) a discussion section relating to the history, mission, and activities of the PN/CHSAA; and (4) a discussion section about the Heirs; relatives of alumni. We included the mission statement of the Heirs as well as the various ways they support the Association. It will be their task to help the PN/CHSAA carry on in the future. The involvement of Heirs also indicates just how much our Hornet nation continues to grow and achieve. Of course, photographs of various events held over the years, including available artifacts, were discussed for inclusion in the overall content of this book. All would be ideal elements needed to enrich even more the story of Carver High School. This book about *Dear Ole Carver High* will be one way to let our story forever be an inspiration to future Hornet generations.

B: The Archives Committee and the Timeline of School Name Changes

The Archives Committee

Robert Jennings, Chairperson, Class of 1960; Georgia Perkins Jones, PN/CHSAA Poet Laureate and Vice Chairperson, Class of 1960; Sandra Burton Barnes, 2009-2011 PN/CHSAA President, Class of 1965; Joyce Adams Shannon, Class of 1965; Susie Larkins Payton, Class of 1970; Julia R. Holmes, Class of 1968; William Holmes, Class of 1967; Gertrude Williams, Secretary, Class of 1964; Linette Fox, Class of 1972; and Willene Coleman Oatis, Class of 1966.

Historical Timeline

Because of efforts by the Archives Committee, various officers of the PN/CHSAA, and individual

*Archives Committee Chairperson,
Robert W. Jennings*

Hornets, a variety of documents, photographs, and artifacts were preserved. As a result, Hornets and the general public will now be able to see photographs of artifacts and learn more about the evolution of *Dear Ole Carver High*. Another interesting aspect of this project is the existence of several versions of the school's history. This turned out to be a blessing in disguise since all of the versions contributed facts not consistently present in each previous version. For example, most versions described the school's origins by saying "the earliest obtainable records" or "from school board minutes". This, however, raised questions regarding which version gave rise to the next. No version examined for this book bore indications of being an update of a previous version. Nevertheless, information from all previous versions led to a composite telling of our school's history. For example, common elements such as names and years of service of school principals and teachers, official decisions by leaders on the local school board, and the location and names of original buildings and their successors have enabled the current version of our school's history to be an accurate representation of Carver High's historical record. It should be mentioned that a contributing factor in all of this relates to the two-year time frame in-between reunion celebrations when different alumni may have taken on the task of writing the history of our school. The important thing now is to thank and acknowledge those who gave their time and effort to prepare the programs which included our school's history. Their combined efforts over the years are a clear expression of how much love and reverence there is for our school. Knowing our history is important. Hornets past and present are intertwined with the experiences had at the "Hive" we call Carver High School. The Archives Committee and all who assisted in their efforts can now receive the credit they so richly deserve.

With this in mind, the timeline below provides a composite view of Carver High School's history as an educational institution that lasted for 80 years (1890 -1970). The name changes are a sobering reflection of circumstances in the Deep South and across the nation as a whole. Additional information is included for historical context only.

Timeline and Context of School Name Changes

1890	The "Colored School" was a two-room wooden building with charcoal heating and no restrooms.
1904	At this time, Pascagoula becomes incorporated. Taxes from liquor sales may imply a new revenue stream for the six square miles (including Scranton) that now defines the City of Pascagoula (see *Pascagoula: Singing River City*, Higginbotham, 1967, pp. 68-69).
1937	Pascagoula High School Colored School (WWII draws nearer).
1938	Pascagoula High School Colored School, in 1939, offering 11 years of schooling. Skip Elementary was built in 1938 and high school classes were taught there as well.
1939-1940	Pascagoula Negro High School offers 12 grades in 1940.
1941	Pascagoula Negro High School's first 12th-grade class. WW II began for the U.S. Between 1938-1941, high school students also went to Skip St. Elementary.
1952-1962	U. S. Supreme Court's *Brown v the Board Education* decision is now law (1954) but virtually ignored throughout the South. In 1952, Carver High School was constructed for grades (7 through 12). An auxiliary tin building was used to teach classes there (i.e., I took 6th-grade classes under Mrs. Christine Cutley and 11th-grade algebra/trigonometry under Mr. Billy Knight in that building). The band hall was completed in 1959-1960 and students no longer used the auditorium at Skip Elementary or its cafeteria (which became the high school's cafeteria) for band practices. Band performances, however, continued at Skip Street Elementary until it was demolished in 1962. Band practice was then held in the new building.
1964-1965	Carver High School's new science building and gymnasium were under construction. The gymnasium was completed first and hosted the District Choir Festival (i.e., I won 2nd place, but other Hornets did better). The new science building was completed between 1964 and late 1965. In May of 1965, my class graduated.

1965-1970   About forty members of the high school class of 1970, who had enough credits, constituted the last class to graduate from Carver High School during the summer of 1970. The remaining members of that class graduated from Pascagoula High School. Although the name of our school was removed for several years, President Jackie Elly and the leadership of the PN/CHS Alumni Association, Inc. convinced the local Board of Education, under Dr. Wayne Rodolfich, to restore our school's name and year of construction. A plaque that was part of the 1952 building is now among many other artifacts saved during 1970. A photograph of the plaque is presented later in this book. Although no diplomas are issued today bearing the name Carver High School, the Tucker St. side of the building has *Carver High School and 1952* (under the name) restored to the building to honor all in the African American community in Pascagoula, MS. Additionally, the Aaron Jones Interactive Learning and Activity Center was named in honor of football, basketball, and Social Studies teacher Mr. Aaron Jones. The music building was named in honor of Mr. Edwin V. Cole and the library was named in honor of Mrs. Mattie Wallace Jennings, Librarian at Carver High School. We are working to similarly add other names worthy of being honored.

Larry G. Hanshaw, Ph.D., History Book Coordinator/Editor-Writer

The History
of Carver High School
1890 – 1970

FROM THE COLORED SCHOOL
TO
CARVER HIGH SCHOOL

**Excerpts From Records and Interviews of the Pascagoula
Negro/Carver High School Alumni Association, Inc.**

CHAPTER 1

The History of Carver High School (1890–1970)

From the Colored School to Carver High School

Records from 1890 indicate that the *colored school* was opened at Saint Mark Methodist Episcopal Church located on what is now Jackson Avenue with Professor W. L. Murphy as principal. In 1904, Scranton and Pascagoula were combined into the city of Pascagoula on July 13. The two-room "colored school" was ready for occupancy. This structure was located on the campus between Skip and Tucker Streets. The campus was bordered on the West by Mr. Frederick Cook's property and

on the east by the two-lane, graveled Market Street. The structure that housed the colored school (below) was eventually turned into a residence for the new principal, Mr. B. B. Jennings, Sr., who replaced Professor Heidelberg in 1939. After the home was moved from its original location on the campus to a location facing Market Street, it became the new Pascagoula Negro High School. The building was eventually sold by the city of Pascagoula which still owned it. The structure is presently located, along with additions and modifications, at 5807 orange Grove Road in Moss Point, MS.

During earlier years, students graduated from the 8th grade and received a Certificate of Completion. In 1923, 9th and 10th grades were added and as early as 1927, Commencement exercises were held, and students received diplomas. The 11th grade was added and in 1940 the 12th grade was added. Records show that the class of 1926 included Charles Leo Durden, President; Dorothy Bessie Barnum, Vice President; Ethel Olivia Smith, Secretary; Leona Margaret Stanley, Assistant Secretary; and Helen Mae Taylor, Treasurer. Other class members were Dexter Lear Cook, Dolores Gladys Boudreaux, and Minolia Marietta Brazley. Their class motto was "Finis Coronate Opus" and the class flower was American Beauty Rose and Fern.

Sometime during the late thirties or early forties, the name of the school was changed from Pascagoula Colored School to Pascagoula Negro High School (PNHS). PNHS offered only 10 grades and 11 grades were offered at Magnolia High School in Moss Point, MS. The class of 1941 was the first to graduate but it was not a class containing only PNHS students. Insightful principal, Mr. B. B. Jennings, Sr., saw an opportunity to help both groups of students receive 12 grades of schooling upon graduation. Mr. Jennings said that if he could get five students to remain after completing the 10th grade, he would assemble a senior class. The Magnolia high school students wanted to graduate with 12 years of schooling as well, so they transferred to PNHS. The students who transferred were Ethelene Wells and Major Owens from Three Rivers, MS. The five PNHS students were: Dorothy Hyde, Armetha Thompson, Alberta Williams, Emma Harvey, and James Carter. These students were considered the first official class because they were PNHS students from the start. The entire graduating class desired to have PNHS class rings which had to be ordered from Herf Jones a company with a contract with Pascagoula (white) High School. All Herf Jones rings read: "Pascagoula High School". This problem lasted as late as 1953. This also created a problem for the U. S. Postal Service. All of "our" mail went to the white school. Daily, a student was sent to Pascagoula High School to pick up our mail. The straw that broke the camel's back happened when new textbooks were delivered to us instead of the used ones we usually got. It is hard not to describe this scenario as nothing short of poetic justice: What comes around, goes around, as the saying goes. Additionally, Professor H. L. Whisenton served as Assistant Principal at PNHS until he became principal at Magnolia High School in the early 1940s. In the class of 1943, for example, were Alva Harvey and Elwood Kimble. In the class of 1944 was Ruth Kimble. Unfortunately, we do not have a complete accounting of entire classes between 1940 and 1950.

A building with asbestos siding was erected in 1938. It faced Skip Street and served as both the high school and, eventually, only Skip Street Elementary School. Skip Street Elementary School was demolished in early 1962. However, during its lifespan, high school students took Home Economics classes there. Additionally, both high school students and elementary grades (i.e., grades 1-6) presented plays in the auditorium at Skip Street Elementary. Parents and the community always packed the auditorium to support all school activities. I recall a womanless wedding and a comedy fashioned around circus characters who sold worthless medicines. My character in the elementary school skit was Dr. Hornswoggle. I smile even now as I think about the nonsense I spoke: "pneumonoultramicroscopicsilicovolcanoconiosis"; got to be good for you for only fifty cents. Step right up ". The word has nothing to do with real medicine but everything to do with comedy.

Mrs. Earnestine Fountain was the principal at Skip Street Elementary for 26 years. She earned her B. S. Degree at Jackson State College and her M.Ed. at Tuskegee Institute. She later held the same position for nine years when Fair Elementary replaced Skip Street Elementary School. Mrs. Fountain was my mother away from home. I could talk to her, as I did my mother, about anything. Both of these women were smart and knew how to instill discipline in children, maximize learning, and help children develop good study habits. Mrs. Fountain's teachers (i.e., Ms. Barrett, Mrs. Chapman, and Ms. Johnson) followed her lead. Ms. Annie Ruth Barrett was my fourth-grade teacher at Skip St. Elementary and taught me a valuable lesson about maintaining one's cool even when bad things happen. Thanks, Ms. Barrett, for doing your job even when I did not do mine. Both Ms. Barrett and Ms. Fountain emphasized letting better students help other students.

Mrs. Earnestine Fountain

This made me feel good about working hard and solving every problem every time. This mindset also stuck with me. I had faith in this strategy and, in later times, during my graduate school years, this early exposure to self-discipline and cooperative learning led me to my dissertation topic. I count that experience as one of the good things in life when history repeats itself. Moving on, a tin-top building near Skip Elementary was used temporarily to provide 6th-grade classes and high school classes. The structure sat behind and perpendicular to Carver High School. As mentioned earlier, I had classes at both grade levels in that building.

In 1952, **Carver High School** was constructed and provided classes for grades 7 through 12. The earliest organized high school band, under Mr. Edwin V. Cole, presented concerts in the auditorium at Skip Elementary. Students did not have a band hall at CHS and, therefore, practiced in both the elementary school's auditorium and for a while in the cafeteria of the high school. Doing so reminded me of my earlier music classes taught by Ms. Juanita Mungen. She too was a particularly good teacher. If I answered all her questions correctly during music class, she would sometimes let me (and/or Ledger Morrissette) go downtown to pay her bills. I loved being trusted by my teacher, but you had better not go anyplace other than where she asked you to go. She was not to be disappointed. Such experiences played a big part in helping me to understand responsibility. Thanks, Ms. Mungen. It amazes me even now how school, home, and church operated under the same rules whenever I faced various challenges growing up. In many respects, I, like others, was well-adjusted to obeying rules by the time I got to Carver High.

Not long after the demolition of Skip Elementary in 1962, a band hall was added to Carver High. A covered walkway connected the band hall and the high school cafeteria. Gone were Skip Street

Elementary School and the adjacent tin building where sixth-grade classes and 11th-grade algebra II and trigonometry were taught. However, a second short-lived tin building was constructed just behind Carver High. It served as the dressing facility for coaches and football players before a new facility was completed across town on the same grounds where Fair Elementary School was built. Head Coach Charles C. Boone and Assistant Coach Aaron Jones led the Hornets during this time. The new brick dressing facility, on the grounds near Fair Elementary, was first used by our football team between late 1961 and the 62-63 school year.

Many individuals shaped the character of students at PNHS. This carried over to Carver High as well. On the staff were maintenance personnel who kept our school clean and cafeteria personnel who kept students well-fed. Many teachers cared for us in various helpful ways, but there were others too. For example, the maintenance personnel included: Mrs. Florence Harris, Mr. Louis Fornett, and Mr. Tinsley Phelps. In the cafeteria were: Mrs. Camille Martin and Mrs. Odessa Wiley. For their service to us and our school, they were honored during a June 2009 program sponsored by the PN/CHSAA. Available photographs are shown for those who never may have known or met these members of the Hornet Family.

Available records list the services of the following Principals between 1939 – 1962: Professor Jones, Professor Love, Professor Heidelberg, Professor Hatch, and Professor P. C. Moore (1938). Moore served before the tenure of Professor Jennings. Professor B. B. Jennings, Sr. served from 1939-1962. Professor C. J. Duckworth, 1962-1963; Professor S. T. Peyton, 1963-1964; and Professor Willie E. Johnson, 1964-1970. All Hornets owe these men a huge debt of gratitude for what they achieved in the face of meager resources and intractable racism. What else better explains the constant practice of supplying schools educating African American students in Pascagoula with used football equipment, outdated typewriters, library books, and few laboratory resources to support instruction in chemistry or biology classes? Regarding the latter, several of my classmates and I often went to the river near the old Puss-n-Boots cat food factory and caught catfish to dissect in our biology class taught by Mr. B. B. Jennings, Jr. Like his father, he found a way to make a way. We thank you, Mr. B. B.! Let me not fail to mention as well the hand-me-down cookware and utensils in the cafeteria. You will find supporting testimony in the interviews with Hornets throughout Chapter 2. Lastly, textbooks were especially egregious. As noted earlier, it was a mistake by the U. S. Postal Service that led to the delivery of new books to PNHS. Nevertheless, when I was in seventh grade, textbooks issued to me were at least a decade old. I peeled back the sign-in sheet within *books* issued to me at the start of school. None of the student names I saw on the pasted-in signature sheet attended Carver High School. In our community, we knew everybody at our school. Since books were issued once a year, many of my textbooks had to be at least a decade old or older (i.e., a year or more for each previous signature). This was in 1959. You will see a similar pattern in (1) the absence of needed resources such as new band uniforms (i.e., the first new uniforms issued in 1959-60), and (2) school district buses (i.e., first used my 10th-grade year, 1962-63). Our first uniforms, for example, were simply black pants, white socks, white tennis shoes, and a long sleeve white shirt complimented with a black bow tie. Our blue and white uniforms came before my ninth-grade year (1961). It is rumored that the above Postal Service error also contributed to the name of our school being changed from *PNHS to Carver High School* to thwart any future mix-ups in mail/textbook deliveries.

I also recall the bake sales and fish fries our parents sponsored to raise money to rent instruments for students whose families could not afford them and/or the uniforms required for participation in the band. I suppose the fact that Pascagoula High School was always in new uniforms with fancy plumed helmets every four or more years left the School Board in a bad light. Our parents paid taxes too. Our teachers and school leadership stood up for us, however, as much as they could. Look back at the time-line. For example, Mr. Cole, our Band Director, refused to have our drum majors, majorettes, and band members march in *any parade* behind horses. You can imagine why. Moreover, Thanksgiving Day and other occasions were special times for our community. Black and white members of the community always lined each street of the parade route. We were showstoppers and knew well musical selections like El Capitan, Simper Fidelis, or any of the other musical scores Mr. Cole selected. We played these selections without the need for brass clamps attached to our instruments. During my time in the band (i.e., sixth grade to twelfth grade), we won numerous district and state awards, trophies, and other competition awards within our school's category (i.e., Carver High at most had only 650-700 students). The PN/CHSAA continues today with efforts to replace what was lost in 1970. The building plaque bearing the name of school district officials and others at the time of Carver High School's construction is presented later in this section. During his administration, Superintendent Dr. Wayne Rodolfich was incredibly supportive of the mission of the PN/CHSAA, Inc. He and his family attended programs spon-

sored by the PN/CHSAA and took part in a televised dedication of the Eternal Flame. It is a large gas light located within a handsomely built, wrought iron fenced area with a small concrete plaza adjacent to the Carver High School gymnasium on South Market and Skip Streets. It symbolizes the undying commitment of all who attended and/or taught at what is now Carver High School. The Hornet family believes that the spirit of all who love our school keeps the history of our school alive and burning within each of us even when the physical *Eternal Flame* is not lit and burning Hornet blue and white. Once again, look at the faces of all those Hornets who did their work so that we could do ours.

In Memory of
Mrs. Camille B. Martin
Cafeteria Manager
of
Pascagoula Negro
and
Carver High Schools

Mr. Louis Fornett.

Mr. Tinsley Phelps

Mrs. Florence Harris

Mrs. Camille Martin

Mrs. Odessa Wiley

Principals P. C. Moore and Heidelberg preceded Mr. B. B. Jennings, Sr. before 1939

In 1970, near the end of the administration of Principal Willie C. Johnson, a notable piece of history was made. Students who were juniors in 1970 received their class rings from Carver High School. They had the choice of graduating in the summer of 1970 if they met certain academic requirements. Otherwise, these students would have to finish their senior year at Pascagoula High School. Half of the class (about forty students) graduated that summer and got their diplomas from Carver High School. Some chose to go to Pascagoula High rather than transfer to another school district. Forty-two black seniors attended Pascagoula High School that year. In so doing, they became the first Hornets to integrate a formerly all-white high school. Later in 1970 and because of integration, Carver High School was merged with Pascagoula High School. Carver High School became for a while the *Pascagoula Annex*. Somewhat later its name and function changed to the "*Opportunity Center*" for problem youth. However, because of negotiations between the School Board (under Dr. Rudolfich) and the PN/CHS Alumni Association, Inc. (i.e., led by President Jackie Elly and the leadership of the association), an agreement was reached which placed "**Carver High School**" "**1952**" back upon the Tucker Street front and Market Street sides of the building. In later years, the Market Street side of the gymnasium bore the name "Aaron Jones Interactive Learning and Activity Center" wherein school-based learning opportunities for young children now occur. The PN/CHS Alumni Association, Inc. is a pioneer among formerly segregated black state high schools for its work to help restore significant elements of the proud legacy embedded in the name Carver High School. Like the symbolism of the Eternal Flame recently dedicated in 2019, the work of all Hornets continues and must not stop now.

The Carver High School Building Plaque

The rich history of Carver High School is filled with anecdotes. One such account details a conversation between an Heir, Mr. Joe Davis, and a school board official with whom he was discussing various matters. The conversation eventually led to a comment that essentially was "I have something in the safe that might interest you". Retrieved from storage was the Carver High School building plaque. CHS alumni are pleased to have this artifact because the information inscribed on it provides construction details pertinent to our high school's history. Be certain to read the "backstory" later in this book. The story explains how close we came to losing this artifact but not why the plaque was removed in the first place. White students received instruction in the same building we did after 1970. The building plaque Pascagoula High School was not removed in 1970 once black students attended this formerly all-white high school.

A key figure due recognition for his support of the PN/CHS Alumni Association and its efforts to advance its mission and purpose is former School Superintendent, Dr. Wayne Rodolfich. His message and support are detailed on the next page and are reminders of the outstanding efforts made by him and his administration during his tenure as District Superintendant. We salute you, Dr. Rodolfich, and wish you and your family success in your future endeavors.

Message from Pascagoula/Gautier School District Superintendent

I would like to say a big thank you to the Carver High Alumni Association and wishing you well on your 2019reunion. I want to thank these members for their faithfulness in service to our children and their diligent work in our community. There has never been a time that we have made the call that it has not been answered by these fine people. It is the Pascagoula-Gautier School District's privilege and pleasure to be a partner with the Carver High Alumni.

We have worked together to create the best opportunities for the children of the community and the Pascagoula-Gautier School District to build a solid future for the young people in our care. We have brought back community pride in the re-development of the old Carver High School. We have worked together to establish an alumni wall and set aside a room for the archives and history of our Carver High School students.

The opportunities we enjoy have grown from a relationship built on volunteerism. The Carver High School Alumni are our largest volunteer organization and have committed many hours in the service of our children during our Super Saturdays. Each year we visit with the alumni and discuss the naming of buildings and how we can advance our efforts to make our community a better place to live.

Please know that our relationship is something we cherish as a school district and one that I personally cherish in getting to learn about the history of this great organization. I am so honored to have been given a blue blazer with the Carver High Alumni Crest on it. Thank you for all you do and we look forward to many great years of working together.

2019 Statement of former Superintendent Dr. Wayne Rodolfich

Extra-Curricular Activities

Football and Cheerleading
Basketball

Football and Cheerleading

Player/Coach Lionel Martin (1940s – 1950s)

Pascagoula Negro High School (PNHS) fielded its first football team in the mid-forties. The first player/coach was Lionel Martin. He was a player/coach during his 10th -12th-grade years. During his senior year, biology teacher/Coach Mr. Patton was hired and coached during Lionel Martin's senior year. Two years later, Mr. Warren replaced Coach Patton.

Coach Alex Warren (1952 – 1956)

Mr. Alex Warren became assistant principal, trade shop teacher, and football coach following the tenure of Mr. Lionel Martin. The team used practice uniforms and castoff equipment from Pascagoula High School (PHS). The team had to use practice uniforms and castoff equipment from PHS. The trade shop was the dressing room, and the practice field was across Market Street where the telephone building and PHS complex are now. Games were played on the PHS practice field on DuPont Avenue where the Central Elementary School is now. At that time, PNHS could not play its games in the city-owned War Memorial Stadium for various reasons. Given the time frame, the reasons are obvious. Visiting teams had to dress in the math classroom of the Home Economics building. It took three years to win the first game. The first victory was against Elizabeth Keys High School of Ocean Springs. The won/loss record was one and eight that year. In all other years, the record was zero and nine. The community, through the PTA, purchase new uniforms in 1950. These uniforms were blue with white stripes and lettering. They lasted until white uniforms with blue stripes and lettering were purchased in 1952 for the game with Magnolia High School of Moss Point. Mr. Warren and his trade shop students built an activity house on the campus to house football equipment and to dress in. Eventually, PNHS was allowed to play in War Memorial Stadium but was not allowed to use the concession area or restrooms downstairs. The reason given was that this area was owned by football and band boosters supporting Pascagoula High School. Given the nature of how expensive such facilities were then (and now), it would be interesting to see official records detailing who the boosters were and how much each one of them paid to control property supposedly owned by the city and paid for with *tax dollars* partly from black citizens of Pascagoula. We have come to learn, that records that might show *"who paid for what"* may have been destroyed by Hurricane Katrina some years ago. However, the racist policies of the time remain the overall reason as has been alluded to above. If not, it would be interesting to hear why black citizens were not allowed the opportunity to share the cost of building the "booster-owned" facilities. Or to construct on the opposite side of the field similar facilities for use by PNHS. Our football players and band members would have enjoyed such facilities as well given the weather conditions on the coast during football season. I know. I played in the band from the sixth to the twelfth grade. From our point of view, there were enough black carpenters, brick masons, electricians, plumbers, painters, cooks, janitors, and others in the city needed to construct such a facility. The city could have picked up other costs of such a project just as they did for the construction of facilities at War Memorial Stadium. Such an arrangement would have been a type of in-kind service. Black churches in Pascagoula would likely have played a part in supporting such costs as part of their traditional building fund efforts. In this case, a building/facility for use primarily by their children and attendees at home football games. Fantasy? Hardly. Who built the black churches in Pascagoula? Restroom and dressing facilities at War Memorial Stadium would have been a walk in the park. So, PNHS accepted the small victory of playing in the stadium and sold their concessions in the stands. Scheduling presented another problem. Games had to be scheduled on Friday nights and Saturday nights only when PHS was playing an away game. A rose by any other name

Mr. Warren also made another outstanding contribution. He penned the words to our first school song. Our first Alma Mater's words are shown below:

Pascagoula dear, we love you, we long for you each day.
Pascagoula dear, we will love you, wherever we may stray.
Pascagoula dear, we love you, we will always stand for right.
We will hold the banner high, the Blue and the White.

During the writing of this book, conversations were held with numerous people who had awesome stories to tell about the efforts to educate and prepare students at PNHS. One such conversation I had was with Mr. J. B. Carter who played quarterback for two years (1954-56) under Coach Warren. Here is some of what he said.

Remembering Coach Warren and His Players

By J. B. Carter, Class of 1956

One of the many outstanding Hornets during the time of Coach Warren was Edward King. King was the most outstanding fullback over four years ever to play at PNHS. King later worked at the Mississippi Press after school and was the best fullback on the coast. Another teammate, Edward Blake, once took the kickoff against one of our rivals (Moss Point) and took the ball to the 50-yard line. On the next play, he took the ball to the one-yard line. As the quarterback, I saw how the defense reacted and decided to try something else. I faked a handoff to Blake and the entire defense buried him on one side of the line. I went the other way and walked in for the score untouched. The second score that night was a pass to Clarence Turner our best receiver. Coach Warren told me how smart I was to take what the defense was doing and use it against them. Edward King became a supervisor helping to print the newspaper in the Mississippi Press print department. Edward Blake became head of security at Ingalls Shipbuilding. Another outstanding player under Coach Warren was Ernest Williams. He was the team's quarterback before I was. Ernest was a role model for me as I learned to play quarterback. Other outstanding players in the late 50s who were stars at Carver High School were: Johnny Jackson, Howard Patton, Marvin Pickett, State Stallworth, Joe Louis Adams, Lionel Barnes, Bobby Pierce,

Clarence Turner, Edward Blake, Glennis Earl (Nick) Barnes, and C. B. Barnes. Other outstanding players were Charles Robinson, Marvin Pickett, Langston Pickett, Ralph Pickett, and Eddie Pickett. At the end of my high school years, I earned a scholarship to Alcorn College but opted to go, instead, to Tugaloo College. Nick Barnes and I were college classmates and worked together at the Colonial Bread Company in Jackson, MS. In later years, I served as the President of the Moss Point School Board and signed my son's diploma in 1977. I will always remember Coach Warren's leadership style as a teacher and coach. He helped to shape the lives of many young men far beyond the football field because he demanded acceptable manly behavior from his players and his students. Shown below is one of the surviving pictures of Edward King, Class of 1953. Another is shown in the reunion photograph in Chapter 3, Part 3, item number five.

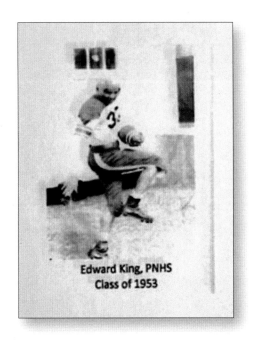

Edward King, PNHS
Class of 1953

PNHS Hornet Football Team of the Early1950s

Coach Warren (Rear, upper left; Principal B. B. Jennings, Sr., Rear, far right)

Basketball

1950 Women's PNHS Hornet Basketball Team

*Bottom: Leoda Manchester, Joyce Crump, Mary Lue Horne,
Delores Cook, and Francis Brown. Top: Earneice Price, Willie Mae
Ducksworth, Velda Kelly, Mary Helen Coston, and Francis Peairs.*

Men's 1950s PNHS Hornet Basketball Team

Recreation Center, Tucker Avenue, Pascagoula, MS

The basketball team of the early 1950s originally had to play outside until the recreation center on Tucker Avenue was built as shown above. The floor of the building was for many years just concrete. A friend and classmate (Edward Hardy) and I earned 25 cents on Saturday mornings during the summer sweeping the recreation floor and cleaning the shower areas. We were paid by Mrs. Eloise Russell who ran the center at the time. The "Rec" was the hub of activity after football games and student-teacher basketball games after semester testing sessions were over for some students. As a sophomore, I played one such game and had fun playing against my teachers (i.e., Mr. Knight and Mr. Pickett). The building has since been renamed the Andrew Johnson Recreation Center and has a swimming pool just behind the building where George Paris, Stanley Moore, George Wright, and I served as lifeguards and taught swimming lessons (1964) as part of the job. I only had the job barely a month before being notified that I was accepted into the Continuing Education Enrichment Program (CEEP) held at Jackson State University. Dr. Jane McAllister ran the program and recruited teachers from nearby school districts to serve as mentors. We were taught Math, Science, and Literature by JSU faculty (i.e., it was Jackson State College at the time). We also visited Tennessee State University, George Peabody College, and Tuskegee Institute. I hated to leave my summer job, but the CEEP experience turned out to be more important because it changed my entire perception of what life was like on a college campus and what was expected of college students. Carver High School had several students take the ACT as part of the selection process. I was happy to be in the group of students from nearby coastal counties selected to participate in the CEEP program experience. Ledger Morrissette, who transferred from CHS to Magnolia High following his sophomore year, was also selected along with Claude McCants who attended Magnolia High School. For now, however, back to PNHS in the late 50s.

Mr. Charles McInnis officiated many games for PNHS. The Magnolia monarchs also played outside on a dirt court behind Chiquita's Inn on Magnolia Street. Elizabeth keys high school in Ocean Springs was the only black school in the area that had a gymnasium at the time.

Pascagoula high school used Greyhound chartered buses when they traveled. PNHS students had to use a bus owned by Pete Green of Moss Point. The reason given was that the chartered buses used by PHS were sponsored by alumni and Panther (i.e., the school mascot) Booster Clubs. Many times, however, bus trips for PNHS were delayed until Mr. Green finished his shift at International Paper Company. He often arrived only minutes before game time. On a few occasions, the windows were broken by overzealous fans of the opposing team. On one trip to Picayune, for example, students were overcome by carbon monoxide gas as they traveled over the Biloxi bridge. After much negotiation, the students were treated and released by a hospital that did not want to admit Negroes.

The Era of Coach Charles C. Boone (1956-1960)

After Coach Warren, Coach Boone led the Hornets from 1956 to 1960. He was a tough coach. Without pads or shoulder protection, I witnessed his efforts to show offensive linemen how to block the defense. He would blow his whistle and at full speed attack the defense. He would then do the same thing on the defensive side of the ball to attack the offense. I can truly say Coach C. C. Boone taught by example. I used to travel on *Tin Lizzy* to the practice area (i.e., near Telephone Rd. on the same grounds where Fair Elementary was later built). My brother, James Hanshaw, played on the team and drove the bus. I got to ride because I would take his trumpet home from band practice. My brother only played in the band for about 30 minutes a day and left band practice to drive the bus to the football practice field. It was only by accident that my mother found out what was going on when a friend of hers mentioned how good my brother played in one of our football games. She had no idea James was on the team. When I was recruited in later years by both Aaron Jones (who served as the Asst. Coach under Mr. Boone) and Mr. Billy Knight, both were told that "someone" is going to play that horn I paid $150.00 for. She never signed the permission slip needed to play and I played the trumpet in Carver High's Band from the sixth grade to my senior year in 1965. Coach Boone also was a man who respected those willing to work. I cut grass during the summer months to earn money. Coach Boone often let me cut his yard. I made certain he was happy with the job before leaving. The Hornet teams, coached by Coach Charles Boone and Asst. Coach Aaron Jones, appear below. Coach Boone is standing next to number 79, Billy Ray Ducksworth, and my brother, James Hanshaw (75) is seated on the ground. Next to James Hanshaw is J. C. Harrison (76) who is in front of Langston Pickett (58) and Robert Norvel (66). Notice as well that future CHS star quarterback and Naval Academy Officer and football star at the academy, **Dr. Calvin Huey (61)**, is on the same team. Coach Boone and Coach Jones are no doubt proud of all the young men they coached. Robert Jennings, in a dark shirt and current Chairperson of the PN/CHS Archives Committee, is standing next to star players Langston Pickett (58) and Bennie Means (63).

Above are the 1956 CHS Hornets led by Coach Charles C. Boone. Hornets are dressed in royal blue and white uniforms, and all brought pride and spirit to Carver High School which was built in 1952. **Coach Boone** [on the end] in the third row next to Billy Ray Ducksworth (79). My brother, James Hanshaw (75), is seated on the ground next to J. C. Harrison (76) and in front of star fullback Langston Pickett (58). Current Archives Committee Chairman Robert Jennings (dark sweater) is standing beside star running back Bennie Means (63). Future Naval Academy star player and officer, Dr. Calvin Huey (61) is standing next to Bennie Means. Star receiver Clarence Turner (65), outstanding running back Eddie Lee Titus

(72), and the heart of the offense, center, Robert Bostic (57) are in the back row. Did I mention earlier how outstanding all of these Hornets played over the years? Well, for good measure, I'm doing it again.!

Trainer: James Marsalis, Robert Martin and Manager Jerald Duffy.

Front Row: Jimmy Rodgers, Alton Pickett, 011ie Walker, Robert Jennings, Jimmy Bradford, Paul Norvel, Willie Jones, George Pickett, and Assistant Coach Mr. Marvin Pickett.

Second Row: Mr. B. B. Jennings, Principal, Willie Fornett, William McElroy , Jake Pharr, Rayford Salters, Joe Tyrus, Robert Thompson, George Williams, Nathaniel Dawson. And Head Coach, **Mr. C. C. Boone.**

Third Row: Charles Fornett, S. B. Brown, Billy R. Ducksworth, Eddie L. Titus, Robert Bostic George Miller, Calvin Huey and James Hanshaw.

Men's 1964-65 (Left) and 1966-68 (Right) Hornet Basketball Teams

The Men's Basketball Teams of the mid to late 60s were coached by Mr. Billy Knight (see also interview responses of Mayor Knight in Part 3, Chapter 2). He was also an Algebra I/II and trigonometry teacher. In addition to being a graduate of what is now Mississippi Valley State University, he is currently Mayor of Moss Point, MS. He is one of the most dedicated teachers and leaders I have had the privilege of knowing. Mr. Knight, the Hornet family salutes you.

The Era of Head Coach Aaron Jones (1960 -1970)

Coach Aaron Jones served the students at Carver High School from 1960-1970. He was simply

more than a football coach. He was active in the community of Pascagoula, MS in summer youth programs and always looked to develop the next generation of leaders and student-athletes. For his service, the PN/CHS Alumni Association, Inc. arranged to have his name on the Market Street side of the high school gymnasium (The Aaron Jones Family Interactive Learning Center). He was my seventh-grade homeroom teacher and taught us civics. To give students an understanding of how society interacts with the law, Mr. Jones took us to the courtroom of Judge Watts. We observed how people received their day in court. He made learning an active and realistic experience. Additionally, to get his students ready for college, he took our homeroom class on a bus trip to his alma mater, Jackson State University. We posted the sign *Seventh Grade Future Seekers* on the side of our bus to let everyone know that we saw the sky as the limit for what we might be able to do if we worked hard enough. A real Hornet who led by example. During the initial efforts of our nation's efforts to launch a man into space, Mr. Jones knew of my interest and aptitude for math and science and asked me to explain to his classes what was occurring when astronaut Alan Shephard achieved his historic suborbital flight into space. I will always be grateful for the opportunity he gave me to let others understand how important space exploration is to the future of mankind. He was assisted by Offensive Coach, Billy Knight, and Assistant Coaches James McIntyre and James Jackson. Their photos are shown below. Note as well two of the star athletes, among many, they coached in the photographs which immediately follow theirs.

James McIntyre   Billy Knight   Aaron Jones   James Jackson

Football

CALVIN W. HUEY

Calvin Huey starred as Quarterback at Carver High School. He then
went on to play Halfback at the U.S. Naval Academy. He was the
first African American to play football for the Navy.

CALVIN W. HUEY   CLASS OF 1961

DEBORAH &   CALVIN W. HUEY

James Marsalis, Class of 1964. Starting Corner for the Kansas City Chiefs in the 4th AFL-NFL World Championship Game defeating the Minnesota Vikings in the last **AFL-NFL World Championship Game** (i.e., now the **Super Bowl**). He was also selected by Pro Football Weekly as the **1969 AFL Defensive Rookie of the Year**. Marsalis played college football for Tennessee State University and played professionally from 1969-1977 (Wikipedia, 2022).

James Marsalis graduated from Carver HS and went on to play for the NFL. He played for both the Kansas City Chiefs and the New Orleans Saints.

CHEERLEADERS 1960-61

"Who are you rooting for?" … Ole - Carver - High!!"

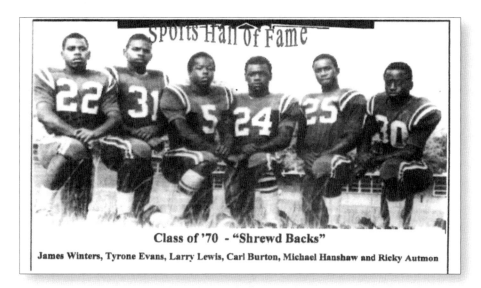

Class of '70 - "Shrewd Backs"

James Winters, Tyrone Evans, Larry Lewis, Carl Burton, Michael Hanshaw and Ricky Autmon

Co-Champs, 1968 Season

Hornet History Nugget Number 1

Don Jennings (Hog)

*Carver High School Class
of 1955-56 Valedictorian*

Achievement: As Team Trainer, Don drew the original design of the CHS Hornet on game-day helmets. Art Teacher, Harris Jr. College, Meridian, MS. A likeness of the **Hornet** is shown in the shield above.

A Skip Elementary/CHS Hornet History Nugget – Number 2

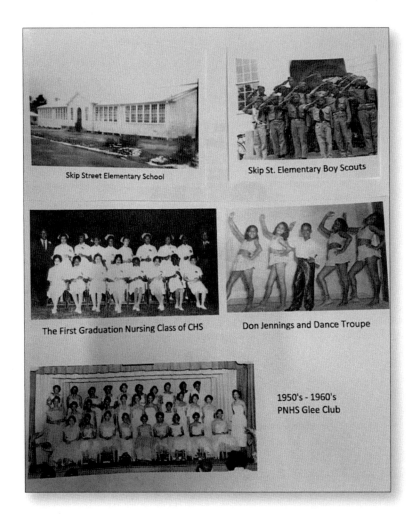

Skip Street Elementary School

Skip St. Elementary Boy Scouts

The First Graduation Nursing Class of CHS

Don Jennings and Dance Troupe

1950's - 1960's
PNHS Glee Club

The first Nursing Class pictured above was started by Dr. Ruben Morris who, at one time, was the only black physician traveling from his office on Market Street (i.e., a building shared with Pharmacist Maceo Dennis) to homes throughout the black communities of Pascagoula and Moss Point.

Music
Band and Choir Faculty at Carver High School

Band Directors

Mrs. Juanita Mungen (Music 1959/(Spanish-1970) and Mr. Edwin V. Cole (1959-1967)

(Information compiled from Archival Records)

Mr. Edwin Vernor Cole was born August 30, 1932, in Ripley, MS. Edwin graduated from Line Street High School in Ripley. Upon graduation, he joined the United States Air Force where he served with the unit that perfected the first hydrogen bomb. After leaving the Air Force, he attended Russ college for a year then transferred to Mississippi Valley State College, graduating with a degree in Music Education. Edwin's first job was as Band Director at George Washington Carver High School in Picayune, MS. He later came to Carver High School in Pascagoula. He was the band director at CHS from the fall of 1959 through 1967. He became a father figure for some of his students. If they had problems, they would go to him. Many students received music scholarships due to his recruiting influence at MVSC (later changed to MVSU by the State Legislature). He was instrumental in organizing ban clinics and competitions between coastal high schools every year. He carried the band to state competitions as well and won numerous trophies. Unfortunately, many trophies, plaques, and awards were destroyed in 1970 due to integration and a complete lack of respect for the hard work of Mr. Cole and the achievements of his band. Moreover, Mr. Cole organized swing bands that performed at clubs and other venues (i.e., the opening of the Morning View Housing Development in Moss Point was one such occasion). Most familiar with Mr. Cole's swing bands will remember the very talented Excel Dorsett on tenor sax who, incidentally, played as well for recording artist Joe Tex. Additionally, Mr. Cole played backup music for some of the popular singers who came to the town to perform.

Although he changed careers, he never lost his love for music. After leaving music he worked with several federal programs. While in Pascagoula, he worked with Head Start and STAR. He later moved to Jackson, MS where he worked with the County Health Improvement Project (CHIP) associated with the University of Mississippi Medical Center. Mr. Cole was united in matrimony with Gwendolyn Daily on December 21, 1957. To this union, four children were born: Cynthia, Nannett, Sylvia, and Edjuana. Mr. Cole departed this life on December 21, 1991; 34 years from his wedding date.

Parents and students who sacrificed their meager resources to purchase or rent instruments or who raised funds from bake sales to pay for instrument repairs or to buy better mouthpieces or reeds using funds from tight family budgets will never forget the dedication and hard work of *Mr. Edwin V. Cole*. The Band Hall at Carver High School bears his name to honor Mr. Cole's legacy at Carver High School. We also will not forget the *heartless acts of destruction* of a large number of artifacts detailing the history of student and faculty achievements across all aspects of extracurricular activities at Carver High School. The leadership of the entire local school board in Pascagoula at the time bears responsibility for what occurred. Although these issues have been discussed and some progress to restore lost artifacts has been made with the assistance of the last school board administration, we look forward to making additional progress with the new school board leadership following the departure of Dr. Rodolfich.

Choir Directors

Mrs. Carolyn Bell Jennings (center and below), Mr. Richard Moore, and Mr. Marvin Pickett

1962-1963 Superior Choir - Carver High School
Director Ms. Carolyn Bell (Jennings) with Championship Trophy

Writers of the (1963-1965) Carver High School Alma Mater

Mr. Richard Moore – Musical score

Mr. Marvin L. Pickett – Lyrics

ALMA MATER

Dear Carver High, we love thee,

Our hearts we give and share with thee.

We'll fight and lift thy name to be,

So that the whole wide world may see.

************REFRAIN*************

Hail to Dear Old Carver High,

Hail to thee, the Blue and White.

We'll Bear thy name through Halls of Fame

• •

And there we'll never be ashamed.

From school to sports, we'll strive for fame,

Our hearts will never ever change.

To our dear school, we pledge our hearts,

Our loyalty will never part.

Science and Mathematics Club Sponsors

Chemistry and Mathematics – Mrs. V. P. Williams Watts, WOF Member

Biology – Mr. B. B. Jennings, Jr. Class of 1953

Bottom Photo: Special to The Pascagoula Press, 2003. Others present in the First row: Lottie Herger Ware, Lenora Barnes Reed, Clarence Johnson Fluker, Ruth Barrett Burney, and June Harrison Slaughter. Second row: Earnestine Price Sylvester, Willie Williams, Oliver Halton, Raife Pickett, Sadie Whitehead Taylor, and **B. B. Jennings, Jr.** Third row: Joe Louis Adams, State Stallworth, Lucille Brown Durden, Helena Joyce Dubose, Edward King, and Alberta Martin Moore. *Reed, Moore, Halton, Stallworth, and Jennings are Wall of Fame Members.*

Hi-Y and Tri-Hi-Y Club Sponsors

Carver High School Hornet History Nuggets (3-4)

*Mrs. Lou Ethel Gibson
Bolton, WOF Member*

Mr. Marvin Pickett, WOF Member

Mr. Richard Moore, WOF Member

History Nugget Number 3

*Mr. James E. Taylor,
Sr., Shop Instructor &
Advisor, Class of 1965*

Mr. James E Taylor senior was born in Meridian MS to the late C. L. and L. V. Taylor. He was a graduate of Mount Selman Elementary School, Webster Junior High School, and T. J. Harris High School in Meridian MS. Mr. Taylor was a veteran of World War II and received an honorable discharge in 1946. After his tour of duty in the U.S. Army, he continued his education at Tuskegee College in Tuskegee, AL. There he received his B. S. and master's degrees in carpentry and brick masonry. Mr. Taylor was employed with the Alcorn Community School District and Booker T. Washington High School in Philadelphia MS. He moved to Pascagoula, MS in 1956 and joined the Pascagoula School District until his retirement in 1987. Mr. Taylor was an active member of the VFW Post 124 and the American Legion.

Mr. Taylor served as the advisor of the Class of 1965. He was also an excellent carpenter and repaired many homes in the Pascagoula community. For example, he added a three-room addition to my mother's home (Mrs. Marguerite J. Hanshaw) on East School Avenue. At the time he was my 10th-grade class advisor. He often joked with me because I built and launched several model rockets (including mice I trained to run a maze for a science project). He encouraged my interest in the U. S. space program. I also cut his lawn as a way of earning spending money. Mr. Taylor was elected to the PN/CHS **Wall of Fame** and the shop area is named in his honor. Be certain to read other comments made about Mr. Taylor in my interview section in Part III. The Class of 1965 provides an Alumni Association scholarship in his honor to support the education of students who wish to further their post-secondary education.

History Nugget Number 4

Mr. B. B. Jennings, Jr.,
Instructor of Biology and
Science Club Advisor

Mr. B. B. Jennings, Jr. earned his bachelor's degree in biology at Alcorn State University and his master's degree at Tuskegee Institute, Tuskegee, AL. He is a member of the PN/CHS Class of 1953 which recently celebrated its 50th year since high school graduation. In 2006, Mr. Jennings was honored for 50 years of service to Alpha Phi Alpha Fraternity, Inc. for the many services he rendered. For example, he served two terms as the Xi Zeta Lambda Chapter's President, associate editor to the fraternity's national magazine, and national and regional convention delegate and director of the coastal district in MS (Mississippi Press, September 13, 2006). He was also, according to the article, very active in working with at-risk male students in the Kreole Elementary School. During my seventh through twelfth-grade years at CHS, I was impressed by the professional way Mr. B. B. dressed and the lab coat he wore while teaching biology. His fraternity sweater also led me to carefully consider my fraternity affiliation as a student at Tougaloo College. I am proud of Mr. B. B. as a teacher and a frat brother. In our biology class, his excellent drawings on the board and his encouragement to us to develop our artistic talent to accurately represent cells, the skeletal structures of animals, the DNA helix, and the human body as a whole made us aware of his desire to do the best job possible even when text-related resources were scarce. Moreover, Mr. B. B., as we called him, allowed several of us to go catch catfish near the Puss-n-Boots factory. The school did not have specimens for us to dissect during biology labs (i.e., finding frogs and garter snakes was no problem either). He nicknamed the females in our biology class "The Nurses". Three of my 1965 class members went on to become members of the nursing and related professions (Frances E. Brown, Peggy Davis, and Joyce Adams Shannon). As a master motivator, Mr. B. B. also provided incentives for high performance each semester of class. For example, he awarded books by Isaac Asimov to students who achieved the highest average in biology. The book I won and enjoyed reading is still in my library to this day.

The Back Story: An Interview with Robert Jennings

Archives Committee Chairman, Class of 1960

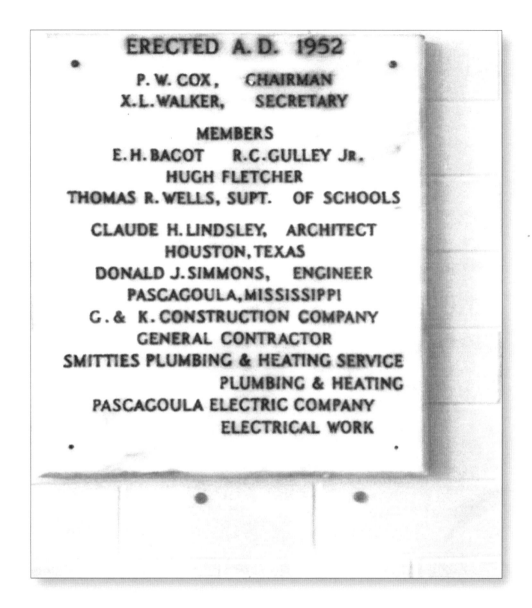

Sometime after the graduation of the Class of 1970, a decision was made by the Pascagoula Board of Education which resulted in the willful destruction of pictures, trophies, awards, certificates, and other records of historical value to the teachers, students, administrators, and parents in the black community of Pascagoula, MS. Were it not for the quick and thoughtful actions of Mrs. V. P. Williams who summoned Robert Jennings, who in turn, got help from Glenn Larkins, Cecil Paris, and others, *none* of what was saved would be here today. The building plaque shown above is just one example of a recently recovered artifact. It is more than just a piece of granite. It is, in fact, equivalent to a birth certificate and adds additional legitimacy to what Hornets already know. Moreover, without a small number of other recovered items, an even larger gaping hole would be left in this present effort to tell our Hornet Nation's story: *The History of Carver High School from 1890 to 1970*. Thankfully, actions by those mentioned above enabled a very different outcome. This book hopes to fill in at least some of our history that was taken away.

From L to R: Jaffus Holloway, Ethel Crear, Berthena Smith, Elbert Wright,
Ann Pickett Parker, Barbara J. Payne, John DeFlanders, and Athersteen Lett.
(Photo: Christy Pritchett, The Mississippi Press, June 27, 2004).

Ethel Crear, Class of 1971, was a member of the first class to graduate from the previously all-white Pascagoula High School. Concerning the plaque presented earlier, B. B. Jennings, Jr., Class of 1953, according to MS Press reporter, Christy Pritchett, said "I hated to see it go" (i.e., Carver High School removed from the building). He also was quoted by the reporter saying "One of the principals, when I was there, said Carver would be there forever. And the first thing that was lost was a chisel knocking Carver High off the wall. It was a very sad occasion" (Pritchett, The Mississippi Press, 2004). Our Association also feels that the local School Board shares the blame for the removal of the *plaque* along with those employees who actually destroyed artifacts and so much more of our school's history. Lastly, those in control at the time and now owe an explanation to the residents of Pascagoula, generally, and especially to its black citizens, regarding decisions that led to the burning of Carver High School's artifacts in several 55-gallon drums in 1970. These containers were brought there by white maintenance personnel who then systematically removed and destroyed part of our school's history. Would it not have been better to let Principal Jennings remove the artifacts? After all, his large photograph that hung in the vestibule of the school over the school's trophy case was among the artifacts destroyed. Why? Alternatively, if any board member(s) or the superintendent in 1970 are still alive today and wish to respond, our Alumni Association will make arrangements to hear their side of the story. Additionally, efforts are ongoing to examine school records that may shed light on this unnecessary travesty.

Over the last decade or so, the PN/CHS Alumni Association, Inc. has managed to recover and replace (i.e., with replicas) some of our school's history. We owe our Mrs. Vivian Williams-Watts, Robert Jennings, Cecil Paris, Glenn Larkins, Joe Davis, the Archives Committee, President Jackie Elly, and our Association a tremendous debt of gratitude for their efforts to restore our school's history. To the extent possible, the Association intends to display these treasures as a way of preserving the history of Carver High School for future generations. Presently, for example, a *secure* location within the Aaron Jones Interactive Learning Center is one location where some artifacts are currently being stored under lock and key. A video recording of holdings also has been prepared.

CHAPTER 2

Voices from the Hive:
Hornet Interviews Help Tell Our Story

Part 1

The Early Years

1890-1929   1930-1934   1935-1939   1940-1944

1. **Interview with Mr. Willie James (Daddy Willie) Smith, Age 103. Interview conducted on June 12, 2022, by J. B. Carter, Daddy Willie's nephew, and Larry Hanshaw.**

My name is Willie James Smith and I now live in Moss Point, MS. I remember arithmetic and spelling and I think it was reading that we also had while I was in school. Most of the children didn't get a chance to go to school because, like me, they had to quit school and go to work to help mama and daddy. That's what I had to do. You didn't get a chance to go to school like children today. A lot of children today quit because they want to quit and get out there in the street and try to make that fast money. We didn't have a chance like children today. My days in school and service to my country have made me even more proud of all I went through. I was recently honored by the Pascagoula/Gautier School District when I received my Honorary Veterans Diploma.

My favorite principal's name was Hatch. I don't remember where he lived but I think it was Skip Street in Pascagoula. Most people taught their children at home. I think as far as I got was the 6th grade or maybe the 8th grade. Most children did well if they got that far. Very few of us got to the 12th grade. Most went to the 8th grade or the 10th grade. I simply can't remember basketball or sports because when we were going to school, helping mama and daddy came first when you came home from school. What I do remember most about school is that for some children teachers would tell them what to do and they would listen. But today, the biggest majority of them out there want jobs paying $20 an hour or maybe $10 an hour. They want to go out there and get this fast money. Fast money is good but if you can get an education that is the best of all. Fast money is all right but when I came out of school the best money was down there at the veneer mill. My cousin was the boss man at the veneer mill and he hired me. A white guy whose name was Ralph was over the entire mill. If my cousin recommended you, Ralph hired you. Besides working in the mill, I had other little jobs too. This white guy who lived not too far from me sold scrap iron. They hired me to stand up there with a note to give to his wife for her to give me a pint or half a pint of liquor. I took the liquor up there to the mill and they would give me a dollar maybe a dollar and a half. I got paid when they got paid. The house that I went to is still there now.

I tell these children of mine that when you went to school everybody was your mama and daddy. If you got a whipping at school, you got another whipping again at home. There was no telephone like everybody has a telephone or a cell phone today. When you got home, if mama whipped you, when daddy came home from work and he felt like getting some, he would not whip you with your clothes on. You got a whipping on your naked behind. These days, some of the older folks would say "I'm going to whip you on your naked ***". My teachers would whip you too, but they tried to do their best to teach you. A lot of them left Mississippi and went to California. I know a couple of people who did leave Mississippi and went to California. A substitute teacher I remember was Dixon Durden who taught as much as he knew. Principal Hatch and another teacher, Naomi Durden, did the same.

When I left to go to the service, there were two doctors around here in Moss Point. One lived in a big house across the street and the other was named Dr. Cale. Whatever they tell you, you might as well put that in the bank. Other people helped me out. I think their name was Delmas. During my time, I don't know if doctors had one, two, or three eyes but whatever they told you, you could take it to the bank. Doctors at that time would do all they could to help you get well. When my sister was in the hospital, who is JB's mother, I would go to the hospital at night at about 11:00 or 12:00 o'clock to see her. I would have a butcher knife that I would stick in my belt. Because if anything had said boo, I would have run away because I was scared that late at night.

When I was working at the mill, Fred Kimble was working there too. You know he had three girls and two boys or three boys and two girls. People back in the day got help to raise their children using the WPA. Whenever children worked, they would get some money, but I don't know how much. They would go out and make that little money and get food and stuff like that. People nowadays get a lot of help using food stamps from the government. And that's what most of them thrive on right now you know. Some won't try to get a job.

Recently I got sick with pneumonia and COVID at the same time. Well, I have problems of my own and I don't know how long I will be here because we can't say how long we gonna be here. That Man upstairs when He says you got to go or you got another two or three years, He may call you upstairs with him. I don't want to go to the hospital unless I really have to. I will go to the hospital to let people do what they have to do to treat me. The rest is in God's hands. OK, y'all take care. You all are a lot younger than I am so look to the Man upstairs that is taking care of all of us. Take care of yourself and all of you be blessed. Thank you for interviewing me.

2. **Interview with Mrs. Ruth Audrey (Kimball) Barefield Pendleton. Conducted by Jackie Elly, PN/CHS Alumni President, June 18, 2022.**

My name is **Ruth Barefield** Pendleton, and I am married to Dr. Pendleton. When I was in school, I was known as Ruth Audrey Kimball. My elementary school years were 1933 and 34 and I graduated from Pascagoula Negro High School in 1945. In elementary school, we were taught English, spelling, and numbers. In middle school, I had English, and home economics, as was required of all students. In high school, I had mathematics, history, English, and home economics. I finished high school in 1945 and was valedictorian of my class. I went to the 12th grade and Pascagoula Negro High School was the only high school in Jackson County. Students from Gautier came to the high school, along with the Catholic kids who graduated from their 8th-grade school. The high school had not been built. Every Friday, the priest would come to our school for two hours and the Catholic kids would be dismissed to go to the auditorium where they would be taught catechism by the priest. I think that should be part of this history. But after the Catholic High School was built in my early years, I thought that was very cool because they could get out of class and go to our auditorium. Back in the early years, Pascagoula was a predominantly Catholic community. All of the officials of the city were Catholics. The mayor of the city was Catholic. So, you can understand why the priest had that privilege. His students could go to the auditorium where he would teach them. Many of them were my good friends but are no longer with us. Mrs. Earlene Durden is my closest friend and is still living there today. She was 95 last October and I was 95 in November. So, we are in our 96th year. But, back to the question you asked. Sometimes I ramble. That is the privilege of an old lady. My school years were influenced greatly by my teacher, Professor Whisenton. He talked about Tougaloo College all the time and that is why I chose to go to college at Tougaloo. When I asked my father, he said boys go to school for education. I said your boys graduated and went to the Army, Navy, and Air Force. I want to go to Tougaloo. My father, Mr. Frederick Kimball, then said if you go to college you should go to Mr. Washington's school. But I said I don't want to go to Tuskegee.

In my early high school years, I could leave my house in the morning, run through the path by the Brooks' house, and in 5 minutes I was in the classroom. And at lunchtime, I ran back through the path home for lunch to use the bathroom because at that time Pascagoula Negro High School had outdoor toilets for boys and girls. That may not be part of this school's history, but you should know it. In school, I was a member of Club 4H: head, heart, hand, and help. Mrs. Wims was our leader and she took five girls to a health convention at Alcorn College. The five girls were all best of friends: Potreen Martin, Grace Hanshaw, Nadine McGinnis, Riva Leroy, and me. The girls from the coast did very well because we scored high in everything. I had three favorite teachers but at different times. Mrs. Naomi Jackson who lived on Harris St taught me in the 3rd grade. Mrs. Esther Williams, I think she was from Hattiesburg, was my favorite teacher when I was in 8th grade. Professor Whisenton was my favorite teacher in the 11th and 12th grades. I taught at Moss Point High School and so did Portrene Morris who also taught Joffrey Whisenton. Principal Whisenton talked of Tougaloo all the time. I was very blessed to have set under his voice. My favorite subject was English. I don't remember it being called Literature, but we had to learn a lot of poems. I loved that because I stuttered as a child. But when I recited the poems, I did not stutter.

During my time in Pascagoula, I worked on the polls. My father registered as a Democrat instead of a Republican as I had suggested to him. Later on, in my career, I wrote a book titled "The Minutes" while working in the civil rights movement in Birmingham, AL. It was published in the 1970s.

As for sports, we had a boys' basketball team and I think there was a girls' team too. We had a boys' basketball team because my brother, Elwood, played on that team along with several others: Cornelius Hanshaw, Leo Reese, Peter Young, Peter Martin, and Leonard Cook. There was also a girls' team: Regina Sabina, Novella Campbell, Emma Harvey, Melissa Willis, and Hattie Willis. I used to shoot hoops with Melissa and her sister, but they were much better than I was. That's probably why they were on the team. Grace Hanshaw and I were very close, even after we graduated from college. Whenever Grace would come through Birmingham, after visiting her daughter, Leah, at Fisk, she would always spend time with me and Barfield. Well, that is all I have to say for now and I will listen to what others have to say. Thank you.

3. **Interview with Mrs. Myrtis Cobb Thomas, June 18, 2022. Conducted by Jackie Elly, PN/ CHS Alumni President, and Larry Hanshaw.**

My name is **Myrtis Cobb Thomas**. I was in high school from 1946 to 1950 at Pascagoula Negro High School. The subjects I studied were math, social studies, home economics, and English. The teachers I remember most were Mrs. Jennings, Mrs. Annie Reed Roberts, Mrs. Cora Dennis (music), and Mr. Cornelius Hanshaw (math). Mrs. Annie Reed Roberts was my best English teacher along with Mrs. Jennings. However, I learned a lot from all the teachers. They would stop by your house or at church to let parents know how you were performing in school. This cut out a lot of discipline problems. One of my best memories was when I went to an oratorical contest in 1949. My dad helped to write a speech entitled "The Negro and the Constitution". It emphasized voting, and what happened to Schwerner, Goodman, and Cheney who were killed.

I got my BS at Jackson State College (now Jackson State University). After college, I taught at Pascagoula Negro High School. We were still paying poll tax then (the 1950s). I left Pascagoula in 1958 at 27 years old and voted in Pascagoula at the time. One very disappointing thing that happened at graduation involved Mrs. Dennis and her supervisor who was a white woman. This woman came to our school and forced Mrs. Dennis to teach us a song for graduation in 1950.

I don't remember the entire song but one of the verses still sticks out in my mind: "Skeeters am a humming on the honeysuckle vine. Sweet Kentucky babe." We had to sing that song for *graduation* in 1950. We hated it. A second incident that we disliked occurred at Mrs. Pauline Brown Young's retirement. She was referred to as "this girl" by then-Superintendent Wells. This was disrespectful to Mrs. Young (or to any black teacher for that matter) who taught PN/CHS students for such a long time. He should have known (or didn't care) how hurtful his behavior was.

I played basketball on Friday nights. I was number 11. Football was played on DuPont St. Robert "Rip" Seaborn, who later became principal at Magnolia High School, was the coach. Mrs. Seaborn taught home economics at Carver High School before going to Moss Point. Besides no new textbooks, which were old when we got them, other conditions were just as bad. I can remember 4 to 5 restrooms connected outside in a row with nothing but a cloth curtain covering the door. Professor Jennings was the principal in 1954 but could do little to build the kind of facilities whites had. Later, I furthered my career as a teacher in Norfolk, VA.

4. My name is **Johnny Ben Blake**. I was born on October 12, 1932. During my school years, I studied algebra, under Professor H. L. Whisenton, geometry, literature, history, and biology. My favorite teachers in elementary school were Pauline Brown Young, Evelyn Johnson, and Victoria Webb at PNHS (then Skip Street Elementary). During my school years, Professor Jennings, who taught shop, took Calvin Patton and me to Eureka High School in Laurel, MS where we entered a shop contest. We rode in his 1946 Ford. We built a set of steps and won second place. I would like to mention that in 1944, Professor Jennings lost his brother Arnette Jennings. He was missing in action. The school was dismissed when the news was announced. The VFW, in Pascagoula at the time, was named after Arnette Jennings. Also, while in high school, Professor Whisenton was my favorite math teacher, Evelyn Johnson was my favorite teacher in elementary school and professor Jennings was my favorite shop teacher.

I played football for one year in high school and then went on to the military where I achieved the rank of Corporal. In high school, we had picnics at the east end of the beach in Pascagoula. Only juniors and seniors attended. We rode on a flatbed truck until all who wanted to attend arrived at the

picnic. Another thing I remember from school was that shots were given by nurses from the local health department. It made our arms sore but kept us healthy. The last thing I would like to mention about school is that the Coca-Cola Company would give us book covers, protractors, rulers, and pencils as gifts. Our books were hand-me-downs from Pascagoula High School. I guess the uniforms were given by our school as a way of making certain that every child had something to wear.

As far as advice for today's youth regarding education, I would say to them: (1) stay in school and (2) go to college. If you don't go to college, get a trade. That way, you will have a lot of control over your future. I look forward to reading what others have to say about the history of Pascagoula Negro/ Carver High School.

Part 2

The Middle Years

1945-1949   1950-1954   1955-1959

1.   My name is **Barbara Joe Payne**. My family moved from McComb, MS to Pascagoula in 1943 when I was in 7th grade. My dad got a job working at Ingalls Shipbuilding Corporation. I attended Carver High School from 1952 to 1954. I got married and then went back to school and graduated. I finished at Tougaloo College in 1979. I taught kindergarten from 1968 to 1980. The subjects I taught were elementary science and adult education. I also taught GED classes to former elementary students. My favorite subject was English, and my favorite teachers were Mrs. Reed, Mr. Warren, who taught math, and Mr. Noblett, who was the football coach. Mr. Noblett also played baseball with the great Jackie Robinson and later worked at Chevron. In the 1940s, my favorite sports were basketball and football. I also recall that we had girls' and boys' teams in basketball.

On a school day in 1945, students were sent back home because of the death of the brother of Mr. B. B. Jennings who was the principal at the time. Mr. Whisenton was hired by Mr. Jennings as our assistant principal. He later went to Magnolia High School in Moss Point. Other teachers that I remember were Mrs. Seaborn, who taught home economics, and Mrs. Camille Martin and Mrs. Christine Miles who were cafeteria managers at what was then PN/CHS. At PN/CHS, we got leftovers: sewing machines, pots, pans, etc. We never got new stuff. Everything came secondhand from Pascagoula High School.

2.   My name is **Alberta Martin Moore** and I was born in 1934. I attended Pascagoula High School Colored School which later became Pascagoula/Negro High School in 1953 when I graduated. It later became more widely called Carver High School in 1955. Mr. Jennings was the principal and Mr. Whisenton was the Assistant Principal and football coach. When Mr. Whisenton left to become the principal at Magnolia High School in Moss Point, several players went with him in 1946. The subjects I studied in school were math, English, social studies, and science (under V. P. Williams-Watts). Mrs. Seaborn was my favorite teacher. In our science classes, we only had two bunsen burners and one microscope. There was not the needed equipment for science classes.

We played basketball and I was on the team and started playing in the 8th grade. I played with the big girls and practiced at the recreation center on Tucker Ave (i.e., the "rec", as it was called). We didn't have a school bus. For out-of-town games, we used a bus belonging to Mr. Green from Moss Point. He was hired by the Pascagoula School system. On one occasion, a dangerous situation developed as we were crossing the Biloxi bridge on our way to a game in Picayune, MS. I passed out. Several others passed out as well. Carbon monoxide was to blame. We were taken to the hospital in Biloxi but because of segregation, they did not want to admit or treat us. We got treated, the game was canceled, and our parents came to Biloxi and picked us up.

We made our uniforms in home economics class. The short skirts were blue, and the tops were white. The first cheerleading squad was Gwen Grand, Sadie Whitehead, Catherine Manchester, and me. In all, there were seven or eight young women on the team. By the time I was on the basketball team in high school, we played our games at the "rec". This was wonderful because most girls older than me played their games outside on a clay dirt court. Barbara Joe Hodges Payne also played a year or so but was behind me. Catherine and I were the best players on the girls' team. My advice to young people today concerning education is that they should examine all available options. Although we are encouraged to go to college, young people today should also realize that everyone is not college material. At the same time, every high school graduate may not be interested in going to college. Many are, however, more interested in learning a trade. Certification in the trade of choice works.

So, if young people today are not going to college, they should choose a trade and complete the training with the highest level of certification possible. Pipefitters, electricians, carpenters, and plumbers are still in high demand. Such fields of employment also offer the opportunity for self-employment in addition to or separate from working for someone else. There is also the field of education. Two of my classmates, Lenora Barnes and Sadie Whitehead, chose to become teachers. I chose to become a Pediatric Nurse Practitioner and spent 20 years working with children who suffered from sickle-cell anemia.

Before I forget this let me mention something else. No matter where you are in this country, I have found that voting is an opportunity to influence the quality of life you may experience throughout your lifetime. The people we vote for are the same people who determine employers who come to the areas where we live in a given state. Electing the right people who pass legislation that attracts a variety of employers gives a broad choice to choose from when you look for good-paying jobs.

Therefore, your vote certainly counts right down to your pocketbook. I voted but not in Mississippi. My parents, however, did vote. They had to pay a poll tax. Questions were worded so that any answer given was incorrect. How many jellybeans are in this jar? Stuff like that. Additionally, the poll tax changed from one dollar to two dollars in this area and others. That was a lot of money for my parents to pay in those days. I am including another picture on behalf of my older sister, Potreen, whom I lost when she was only thirty years old. The picture shows her son, Kenneth, and me. Thanks to you and Jackie Elly for interviewing me. I have enjoyed contributing to the important history of our school.

3.   My name is **Lenora Barnes Reed** and I am a 1953 graduate of Carver High School. I took all the required courses to graduate at that time. I am also a graduate of Jackson State University. After college, I taught U. S. History at Carver High School. In addition to textbook assignments, I often integrated into class discussions a current events publication that emphasized world events. This enabled students to learn about politics, other governments throughout the world, and our country's posture toward events occurring in other nations.

I coached cheerleaders at Carver High and taught values related to physical fitness, loyalty, and being mindful that win, lose, or draw, one's behavior will be a reflection of your school and family wherever one might go. No one is perfect, but it is worth it to be the best person you can be throughout life. Students probably received these messages about good citizenship in every class at Carver High School.

I am a member of the PN/CHS Wall of Fame. I support its scholarship efforts which will help the next generation of Hornets achieve an education beyond high school. My advice to students of today is to stay in school and get the highest level of education possible. There are also opportunities to learn a trade of choice. Either pathway may prepare you for life's challenges in today's world. There are also many apprenticeship programs to consider. Choose whatever best fits your dreams and abilities. Involve God in your life and he will guide you to achieve whatever you seek.

4.   My name is **Marvin Leon Pickett, Sr.** I went to Skip Street Elementary School during the time that the wood-framed building was there. Later, Skip Elementary was built. My early school was a wood-framed building heated by wood with outside toilets for boys and girls. We had a basketball court outside on red clay dirt. I took geography, math, reading English, and spelling. During high school, I studied trigonometry, English, math, and chemistry (under V.P. Watts). She was responsible for my going to Tougaloo College on a music scholarship but later I majored in sociology under Dr. Ernst Borinski. Mattie W. Jennings, who addressed me as Mr. President, taught me English and current events in her class. Mr. Warren was my football coach and shop teacher. Mr. Jennings was the principal at that time and later offered me my first job at Carver High School. The job brought me back home to Pascagoula after graduation from Tougaloo College. I was valedictorian of my 1954 class in high school at PNHS. The name changed officially around 1958 to Carver High School. My favorite subjects in high school were English and math. I recall that our first high school play was entitled "He Couldn't Take It". It was presented at Skip Street Elementary auditorium. Betty Ruth Ducksworth was also in that play.

On our high school football team, I played right tackle. Three other brothers played at the same time. Raif played center, Edward played left guard, and Langston was a running back. We played our football games on DuPont Avenue where Central Elementary School is now. War Memorial Stadium was not built at that time (1951-52). When we graduated from Carver High School in 1954, the stadium was practically new. We were not allowed to use the restroom facilities at War Memorial Stadium. We had to relieve ourselves at the end of the stadium field or go back to the school campus at the Hornets' Nest to use the bathroom on campus at PNHS. This was before the 1954 Board of Education decision.

We had parades and I was a parade captain for one year. During that parade, I used Eric Thompson's scooter as the Parade Marshall. I had a slight mishap when I gave the scooter too much gas during the parade. I was not seriously injured. Pep rallies and hayrides were related activities during my high school years and afterward. While a teacher at Carver High School, Omega Psi Phi Fraternity sponsored a talent show, and my sister, Lou Ann Pickett (Stroman), won first place on one occasion. She is now retired from the field of opera and teaches music at home in Georgia. I also was a lead sponsor of Hi-Y Tri Hi-Y Club activities at Carver High School. We traveled all over the state to enable CHS students to participate in Hi-Y and Tri-Hi-Y activities. On one such occasion, we were stopped and given a ticket, but we were not speeding. After the ticket was paid, the white court official said, "go thy way and sin no more".

I offer the following advice to students regarding education: (1) select your peers/associates who strive to accomplish worthwhile goals; (2) select role models/people you would like to follow or be like someday; (3) let your learning in school be meaningful; (4) select a vocation and work towards achieving it and (5) Always practice being respectful and courteous to your peers who try to help you to succeed.

5. My name **is J. B. Carter, Jr.** The subjects I studied were math, English, history, and geography. During my elementary school years, I completed pre-primer, primer, and then first grade. I attended Skip Street Elementary School from 1943-1952 and Carver High School from 1952-1956. Some may not know that part of the time, Skip Street Elementary School also was used by high school students who took classes in some of the rooms.

What I remember most about my school years were: (a) Shop (carpentry and brick laying); (b) football; (c) my high school prom; (d) my 8th-grade graduation ceremony; and (e) my high school graduation. While in high school, there were 13 students in my graduating class. Jeanette Williams was the valedictorian; Jacqueline Patton was the salutatorian, and I was the class historian and graduated with the third-highest average in my class.

My favorite teachers were V. P. Williams-Watts, B. B. Jennings, Sr., and Ms. Ophelia Evans. Football, basketball, and track were also a part of my school experiences. Mr. Warren was our football coach and shop teacher. During coach Warren's tenure, football players had to bring him cigars before boarding the bus. In one game, to beat Waynesboro, I threw two touchdowns to Clarence Turner. In another game against Biloxi (Nichols High), Edward Blake was in the game in place of Bobby Pierce, the starting fullback. Edward Blake ran the ball 99 yards down to the 1-yard line. On the next play, Nichols High players thought Edward was going to run the ball. I faked the hand-off to Edward and scored on a quarterback sneak…untouched. Edward has not forgiven me to this day (smile). I often told him he took one for the team. Coach Warren thought that I was pretty smart to have understood what the defense thought.

The *graduation diploma* my mother earned has always been a very special source of inspiration to me. I lost her very early in my childhood, but I stayed in school and lived alone in my grandmother's house for about three months before going to Tougaloo College. I have included my mother's diploma as part of my statement.

I also share with you my eighth-grade graduation picture because it inspired me to reach many other goals. One of the many things that I learned during my youth came from those early years when at times good advice was hit and miss. With the help of my uncle, Daddy Willie (see the first interview I helped conduct with Larry Hanshaw), I hung on to certain sayings that helped frame my understanding of the world. One such saying was "A lie will travel around the world while the truth is lacing up its boots".

I graduated from Tougaloo College in 1960 just over twenty-five years after my mother graduated from high school. I know she is proud of me. During my time at Tougaloo, I worked at the Colonial Bread Company in Jackson, MS with my college roommate and best friend, Glennis Earl (Nick) Barnes, also a Carver High School graduate.

Before the PTA or PTO, we had what I like to call the PCTC: **P**arents, **C**hurch, **T**eachers, and **C**ommunity. All of these components came together to support the schools we attended. Parents taught their children how to read and write their alphabet before they started school; the church provided the podium for public speaking; teachers at school taught many of the same parental teachings and broadened our knowledge; and the community supported the principal, teachers, and students in all of the school's activities.

My advice to today's youth is the following: Education is not an option. It is the "open sesame" to the world. So, get an education! The last thought I share with you is also a source of pride for me and my family. When my son graduated from high school in Moss Point, I signed his diploma as the School Board President.

Eighth-grade graduation picture of J. B. Carter.

6.   My name is **Jerry B. Blake** and I graduated from Carver High School in 1957. The subjects I studied were first- and second-year algebra, geometry, biology, chemistry, history, government, civics, literature, English, drama, health science, and physical education. My favorite teachers were V. P. Williams-Watts (science and math), Cornelius Hanshaw (social science), and Mattie Wallace Jennings (English and literature). Mrs. Jennings had a great love for literature and insisted that all her students learn the last verse of William Cullen Bryant's poem, *Thanatopsis,* which I still can recite to this day. Two other teachers I remember from my elementary school days were Ms. Myrtis Cobb and Mrs. Pauline Brown-Young. Ms. Cobb taught English at Carver High in the 1950s. Mrs. Young was my fourth- and fifth-grade teacher. I will always remember her interesting geography classes. Mrs. Young taught elementary school in Jackson County for over fifty years. I would also like to mention a few of my school classmates who were a couple of years ahead of me. I believe Norma Jean Patton and Dorothy Mays-Boston are still living. Dorothy was married to Ralph Boston, the famous Olympic track star from Laurel, MS. I do not know Norma's married name, but I can probably get it from her cousin, Mattie, here in San Diego. So, as far as I know, my brother, Johnny (whom you are scheduled to interview), Dorothy, and Norma Jean may be the only living 1951 graduates.

Jerry Blake and niece Lisa M. Ellis-Porter

Others in the 1951 graduation class along with Johnny were Roland Farmer, Bennie Massie, Amzie Waters, Dorothy Mays, and Maxine Barnes. There are probably five or six others I did not know well who still may be with us. Professor Whisenton was their high school math and science teacher during that era.

Mrs. V. P. Williams-Watts taught me math and I will always remember when she introduced us to Venn diagrams. This sparked my interest in mathematics. Concerning sports, Johnny Jackson and I shared quarterback duties on the 1956/57 Carver High School football team. One of our greatest victories was defeating Oak Park High School of Laurel, MS. Oak Park had not lost a game in three years and was considered one of the best high school football teams in the state at the time. I have sent you a few other photographs I hope you will use because they show classmates, alumni, and former football teammates others may wish to know are still with us. In the next photograph, *my wife, Rosana*, and I are at the St. Joseph College Alumni Celebration, The Philippines.

My advice to the youth of today: Believe in yourself and everything will come to fruition at the appropriate time. You are unique and special in the way you are. You are lucky to be alive at this time in human history. Let nothing stop you from what you want to achieve.

Rosana, Brandon, and Jerry Blake, UCLA Family Day

*Below: Vonita Blake-Ellis (CHS Alum)
and daughters Lisa M. Ellis-Porter
and India Ellis-Bolden*

L to R: J. C. Harrison, Annabelle Dennis, Mattie Henry Jackson, and Jerry Blake, Class of 1957.

Pallbearers at the funeral of CHS classmate Barbara Jean Joyce, Class of 1957.

NO.	NAME	POS.	WT.
62	Barnes, Charles	G	165
64	Barnes, Glennis	B	145
67	Baringner, Earle	E	196
57	Bostic, Robert	C	185
59	Costic, Willie	G	150
28	Blake, Edward	B	170
50	Blake, Jerry	G	164
73	James, Willie	G	201
26	Moore, Donald	E	175
54	Marshall, Sims	C	162
25	Duckworth, Billy	T	171
66	Robinson, Edsel	T	160
63	Means, Bennie	B	175
52	Harrison, John	E	151
22	Pickett, Alton	G	160
72	Taylor, Robert	T	175
60	Jefferson, Jerry	E	160
65	Turner, Clarence	B	155
58	Pickett, Langston	B	160
68	Martin, Jessie	G	195
53	Webster, Jimmy.	B	145
56	Rogers, Fred	T	185
70	Richardson, Clarence	T	190
51	Jackson, Johnny	B	155
71	Stafford, Uranus	B	150
61	Patterson, John	T	170
24	McElroy, William	T	196
33	Turner, Joe	B	145
32.	Pharr, Jake	G	150
17	Lett, Roosevelt	E	140
30	Payton, John	E	155

The roster lists the names of CHS football players and their positions. **From L to R** in the photograph of pallbearers are James Winters, Edward Blake, Roosevelt Lett, Fred Rogers, Edsel Robinson, C. B. Barnes, John Patterson, Jerry Blake* , and Johnny Jackson* (*Blake and Jackson shared quarterback duties on the 1957 Carver High School football team). The picture was taken at Asbury AME Church, Pascagoula, MS (circa) 1991/92.

7.   My name is **Lillie Bohannon Wright**. In 1957, I graduated from Pascagoula Negro High School. My class was the last to graduate from the school by this name. While in school I studied English, algebra, geometry, and home economics. Mrs. Young was my favorite teacher. Her class was the last class to graduate from Pascagoula Negro High School. I went on to study at Virginia State University for two years and later I became the first black employee at City Lumber Company in Pascagoula, MS. I worked there for 32 years and integrated the staff. Several people there took me under their wing. I worked up to stocker and from there to cashier. From that position, I became a salesman. Later, I became the first black contractor salesman at City Lumber Company in Pascagoula. Concerning voting, I voted in 1960-61. A white man named Ramsey managed the voting process at the time.

Basketball tournaments were held on 14th St when I was at Pascagoula Negro High School. I helped to make our history at that time. I also wish to mention that Ms. Wims was my 4-H Club sponsor who taught us a lot.

8.   My name is **Earnestine Barrett Cook** and I married Emile Cook. The subjects I studied were math, English, science, social studies, physical education, and music. My favorite subjects were math, English, and music. I attended some of the Hornets' football games during the school year. Also, I enjoyed being part of the Glee Club and singing at talent shows. My advice for today's youth is to set goals for themselves, stay in school, and listen to what their teachers are teaching and saying.

9.   My name is **James Parker**, and I was born in 1942. I graduated from Carver High School in 1958. I studied math, shop, history, and English. The things I remember most about my school years were (1) going to different schools for workshops to improve my shop skills (2) meeting new students each school year, and (3) going to Pascagoula High School for a shop meeting with their shop students. They had everything we had and a lot more than what we had. For example, they studied pipe fitting, welding, mechanics, carpentry, brick masonry, and other stuff that enabled them to get jobs out of high school. I also remember preparing for graduation and the tests needed to graduate. My favorite subject was English, and my favorite teacher was Miss Lola Bell who taught typing. Mr. B. B. Jennings was my favorite principal. Sports were also a part of my school experience. I played quarterback on the football team. I also enjoyed basketball and baseball. While playing quarterback for two years, we beat Newton 19 to 0. They had not lost a game. I threw two touchdown passes to Clarence Turner.

My advice to students regarding education is this: Every student should study to obtain an education. They should also study their Bible and accept Jesus as their Savior. He will be with you in all your studies. To do your part, you must stay in school and learn all that you can. Be a good student and respect your teachers. They have what you need.

James Parker, Class of 1958

Part 3

Years of Change, Destruction, and Restoration

1960-1964   1965-1969   1970 and Beyond

Civil Rights. Voting Rights. Schwerner, Chaney, and Goodman.

School Busing. March On Washington. Black Panthers. Sit-Ins.

Deacons For Self-Defense. Freedom Summer. Birmingham Civil Rights Institute.

Malcolm, Martin, John, Medgar, and Bobby. Selma, AL. Fisk University.

Farrakhan. SNCC. CORE. Fanny Lou Hamer. Lorraine Hotel Museum.

Voter Registration. North Carolina A&T. Jackson State. Freedom Riders.

SCLC. Memphis Garbage Workers' Strike. Ole Miss. James Meredith.

Birmingham Bus Strike. Tougaloo College. 16th Street Baptist Church.

… and so much more.

*"Ain't Gonna Let **Nobody** Turn Us Around"*

1.   **Interview with Mr. Billy Knight, Sr., Mayor of Moss Point, MS. Interview conducted on September 5, 2022, by Larry Hanshaw.**

Mr. Billy Knight, Sr. and his wife,
Retired Principal Lois Knight, at
the PN/CHS Alumni Ball

My name is **Billy Knight, Sr.** and I joined the faculty at Carver High School from 1960 to 1970. I am a graduate of Rowan High School in Hattiesburg, MS, and Mississippi Valley State University. I taught mathematics at the junior high school level and algebra 1/2 and trigonometry in grades 10 through 12. I was the assistant football coach for the offensive team and called the plays. I also was Carver High's basketball coach. During my time at Carver High, I had to fight for many of the same provisions already given to Pascagoula High School. For example, students needed slide rules for math and chemistry classes but Pascagoula High School and school board officials refused to share even the excess supplies on hand. Consequently, advanced classes requiring slide rules and other supporting supplies were not offered because white school system officials simply did not want advanced classes offered at Carver High even though I and other teachers were more than capable of showing students how to use such school supplies. It was well known that there were more advanced degreed faculty in science and math at CHS than at PHS during my time at Carver High.

Our relationship with colleagues and students at Carver High was close-knit. All the teachers went back to school in the summer to stay abreast of the latest changes in the subjects we taught. This kept our students up to date in the subjects offered. Many of us earned master's degrees during the summer and advanced ourselves because we wanted to be qualified in every subject taught, or potentially added in the future, to the CHS curriculum. We also had very supportive parents who were available to work with their students and teachers. Parents raised funds to purchase school supplies and some of the equipment needed in the classroom. For example, copy machines (i.e., Xerox machines) were purchased along with bunsen burners for the chemistry lab. Five hundred pairs of white pants for football were purchased and half of them were dyed blue and used on game day. A homemade blue and white stripe was added to the game-day pants to distinguish game uniforms from practice uniforms. Home economics volunteers sewed stripes and cloth purchased by parents. This help was also a learning opportunity for home economics students which also supported CHS athletics. In basketball, all games were away because CHS had no gym. Pascagoula High officials would not let CHS coaches/players use their gym even though they were out of town at games elsewhere and could have let us use the vacant facilities. The parallel here, of course, is the use of War memorial Stadium when Pascagoula High was out of town. CHS coaches offered to schedule home games around PHS's schedule when their gym was not being used. They refused. Like basketball, football teams were not any better. Halftime visiting teams and CHS players could not use the dressing room facilities under the stands at War Memorial Stadium. We gathered at the end of the field and/or under the stands at halftime. Perhaps school officials at PHS didn't want CHS players or coaches to see "exactly" how unequal their support for athletics was between PHS and CHS. Nevertheless, black parents were not exempt from paying taxes in Pascagoula.

This situation was not confined to high school athletics. It also occurred at the college level across the South in many instances (i.e., Florida A&M in Miami and Texas Southern University in Houston, TX). Hand-me-down shoulder pads, helmets, shoe cleats, and repair kits for shoes and shoulder pad equipment were repaired by trainers on the team to make the equipment safe for use. This was as true at the college level as it was at the high school level. College and high school coaches compared notes about how they were being supported just as high school players did often at the end of games or conference meetings. Regardless of level, new shoes were a novelty while used equipment repaired for safe use was the norm. Helmets were painted by team trainers going back as far as Don Jennings, James Marsalis, and many others.

Integration had many unintended consequences. For example, dropout rates increased dramatically after integration. It was nearly rampant at CHS. Teachers and parents communicated frequently about school attendance and academic achievement because parents wanted to know how their children were doing in school overall. Teamwork got the job done for parents and teachers. Back in the day, teachers socialized with other teachers at their homes and did not frequent the same places as parents. School principals did not allow faculty to do this. Teachers and parents were dedicated to improving students and supporting outcomes expected of them by principals and parents.

Additionally, I was an active sponsor with the Hi-Y and Tri-Hi-Y and student government/student council organizations. In later years as Mayor of Moss Point, I asked Delta Sigma Theta Sorority to help tutor today's school children to help them respond to questions they had during a speech I was asked to deliver. I also discussed how school organizations could prepare young people for leadership roles in life. The school organizations mentioned previously and church organizations taught these same skills so that in later life students would be able to prepare themselves to become leaders. This helped students to know important information about certain roles of leadership and what these roles would look like.

My advice to students today regarding education is the following. Stay focused on each subject. All subjects are important. Take the attitude that all subjects are important because you may need each of them. It is always better to have and not need than to need and not have. Moreover, be willing to put in the time for all subjects. There is no substitute for studying and preparation. Like a step ladder, every wrung on the ladder is there for a reason. Hit each one on the ladder along your life's journey because every step will count to complete your career. What you miss may be the very thing that may cause you to have less success than you are capable of achieving.

2. My name is **Richard Moore** and I am a 1957 graduate of Nichols High School in Biloxi, MS. I came to Carver High School in 1961-62. I majored in Music/English (i.e., nearly a double major) and graduated from Jackson State University. In 1967, I earned my master's degree at Tuskegee University. Students in my 9th-grade class kept me busy because they were so smart. I loved the challenge of keeping everyone on their toes. I took extra time with other students who needed extra help. Marvin Pickett and I (our *photographs* were shown earlier) had music backgrounds. We got together and I wrote the musical score and he did the lyrics between 1963-65 for the high school alma mater. In 1963, I took over choral music and soloed on a program in Mobile, AL. Our choral group received an Honorable Mention in our district. We competed only against schools with similar school populations. Carver High School, during my time there, had only 600 to 700 students. We competed at the state level and sang songs that other similar-sized schools sang. George Pickett won first place locally and won a trip to Miami, FL where we competed in a talent contest sponsored by Omega Psi Phi Fraternity. The fraternity paid for the trip. I also remember saying to students I worked with "if you can talk, I can teach you to sing". Additionally, I played for several Pascagoula churches: Union Baptist, St. Peters (on the beachfront), and Asbury AME Church. I also played and directed music at my home church, First Missionary Baptist in Biloxi. Linda Martin, Margie Joseph, Dorothy Rollins, and Delores Hardy sang in a small group whom I worked with. Mary Goode, in 1967, was in the choir in my homeroom when she was crowned Miss Carver High. Pageant contestants had to perform wearing evening gowns, casual wear, and a talent rendition. I also worked with other students to avoid partiality. Additionally, I mentored Leah Travillion who was very talented in music and singing. Mrs. Lucas (our Home Economics teacher) and I also took students to Tuskegee to see the campus. Carver High School teachers earned master's degrees paid for by the International Paper Company here in Pascagoula. This put pressure on PHS teachers to earn M.Ed. and M.A. degrees. Many refused and quit in favor of jobs at Ingalls Shipyard. It was not always about the money.

Since I began teaching, education has changed. Students then were eager to learn and they worked hard. Not so much today. Some seem not to have the same aspirations as students did when I was teaching. I think the problem is at the doorstep of parents who are, for whatever reasons, not as strict about education as in the past. More involvement on the part of parents needs to be a significant part of the lives of today's youth.

I heard about the recent Smithsonian Voting Exhibit held at Pascagoula High School. It brought back memories of what I and others went through. In the sixties, teachers were required to read and interpret a passage from the state constitution to vote. Teachers also paid a $2.00 poll tax in 61-62. This was required and other people, namely blacks, could not vote at that time. Officials administering these requirements also had the power to choose who would pass or fail. This was voter suppression by any other name. The Mississippi poll tax was declared unconstitutional by a federal panel on April 8, 1966. I have enjoyed being interviewed by Larry Hanshaw, one of my top ninth-grade students whom I also worked with during his senior year for a 1965 district choir festival held at Carver High School's new gymnasium. He did well but won 2nd place. I look forward to reading the experiences of others in the upcoming history book about Carver High School.

3.   My name is **Georgia Perkins Jones** and I am a 1960 graduate of Carver High School. I attended Mrs. Dora Cook's kindergarten before going to Skip Street Elementary School. The subjects I studied in high school were English, biology, history, home economics, and algebra. No college prep classes were offered at the time I was in high school. However, I had top-notch teachers. Mr. Coleman was one of my favorite teachers. He gave me a D in math which I deserved because I lollygagged too much in school. However, after that grade, I got my act together. Other favorite teachers were Mrs. Cobb and Mrs. Lou Ethel Gibson who taught English. I was babysitting Mr. Aaron Jones's son when airman Cobb (a CHS graduate) flew over our neighborhood on School Street and dipped the wings of his plane. That was an event that many in the Pascagoula community cheered on and will never forget because it was performed by a skilled black airman stationed at Keesler Air Force Base in Biloxi, MS.

I have written poetry for our alumni association and many others. I am the current Poet Laureate for the Pascagoula/Negro Alumni Association, Inc. My enormous love for poetry stems from the two ladies I just mentioned. I am currently in the process of getting my first book of poetry published. Mrs. Cobb (now at age 96 and still sharp) said she would buy the book whenever it goes on sale. My favorite principal was Principal B. B. Jennings. He was a very understanding person and a capable administrator who cared about the students at Carver High. For example, Mr. Jennings once caught Frozine Larkins, Barbara Moore, and me trying to skip school. All he did, with arms crossed, was say "ladies, go back to class", which we did. We learned to respect our teachers because of the way they treated us. In school, I was part of the choir, the Glee Club, and a cheerleader because I had a loud voice. Mr.

Alex Warren was our coach at the time along with Mr. Boone and Mr. Jones. Later on, Carver High had a basketball team but I did not play sports or go to many basketball games.

Teachers wanted us to finish school and go to college or trade school so that we could live productive lives. This same advice is what I give to students of today so that they might be successful in whatever careers they might choose. In addition to the quality of life each of us might desire or how it might best be achieved, I am also concerned about voting. Everyone should vote. Without exercising this power, others will vote and their desires and decision-makers may not be the mayors, city council people, governors, representatives, senators, or federal government officials who will justly address our collective needs. If you don't vote, don't complain. Legislation that gets passed is done by those we elect. My participation as a panelist in the Smithsonian Institution's Voting Project, held recently at Pascagoula High School, was an opportunity taken by me and other panelists from both Carver High School and Magnolia High School to emphasize our concerns about this very important civic duty. Many of us spend hours at a football game, restaurant, club, or casino. All of the things just mentioned are choices. Make another choice and take the time to vote. The audience enjoyed our collective comments and the Smithsonian program organizers thanked us for helping to emphasize the history and importance of voting.

4. My name is **Ann Tyrus Pickett-Parker** and I am a 1960 graduate of Carver High School. The subjects I studied in high school were English, history, math, business courses, home economics, biology, and chemistry. I also was a majorette in the band (led by Mr. Cole) and sang in the CHS choir. Several of us were members of the Johnny Mathis Fan Club. Classmates Corine Hanshaw, Shirley Barnes, and Valetta Thompson performed in a group we called the Silhouettes. I guess we learned even more about performing in public after we went to see Nat King Cole at Ladd Memorial Stadium in Mobile. We sat on the opposite side of the stadium with whites who were present and all of us wore white outfits and white gloves. Some of the other things I remember most about my school years were my participation in 4H Club activities, attending football games as a cheerleader, and performing lab experiments in chemistry and biology. Chemistry was so exciting because of Alton Pickett and Calvin

Huey. We were so adventurous when it came to performing experiments, sometimes without the specific equipment needed. We improvised and learned as much as we could even without all of the chemicals and equipment we simply did not have. Sock hops were a lot of fun as well but we learned a lot about the importance of school at assembly programs. I also enjoyed my time in the library and my participation as a member of the girls' basketball team from eighth to tenth grade.

My favorite principal was Mr. B.B. Jennings, Sr. I will always remember him for his kindness, mercy, and understanding. In 1958-59, I was crowned Miss Carver High. I was also secretly married to Langston Pickett on my sixteenth birthday. Mr. Jennings knew of our marriage. One might also say that I was (secretly) Mrs. Carver High. Mrs. V. P. Williams-Watts was one of my favorite teachers. She was also a very wise person. I enjoyed the way she taught chemistry (my favorite subject) and mathematics. In some ways, I believe being taught by her led to my decision to become a teacher of eighth, ninth, and tenth-grade mathematics at Carver High School in 1969. Other teachers who were favorites were Mr. Marvin Pickett, Mrs. Mattie Wallace Jennings (school librarian at the time), and Mrs. Juanita Mungen who taught seventh-grade music in the cafeteria before the arrival of Mr. Edwin Cole.

Concerning education, my advice to young people is that they ask God for wisdom to do what they need to do now. Realize that there is never a "right time". Have a purpose in life and think positively. Waiting will only make you older, not wiser. Don't blindly accept the status quo or be a lemming. Have goals and don't let others upset you or steal your power of self-determination. Lastly, don't try to change people or be too quick to judge others.

5. My name is **Shirley Beatrice Barnes Laird** and I am a 1960 graduate of Carver High School. The subjects I studied were English, social studies, biology, math, chemistry, and home economics. I dropped home economics because I wanted to sew clothes, not aprons. I did eventually learn how to sew. Some of the things I remember most from elementary school related to some elementary teachers who were nosy and always tried to get information from me about my family. I also remember how competitive the students were and how some teachers had pets. I never developed those attitudes once I became a teacher. In high school, Miss Lou Ethel Gibson and Mrs. Mattie Jennings were my favorite teachers. My favorite subject was English. I liked Professor Jennings who was my principal. I was an office aide and Nettie Ruth Ducksworth was the secretary. We always had snacks to eat even if I had to go to Thornhill's Grocery Store on Market Street to purchase them.

My sister, Lenora Barnes Reed, was over the high school cheerleaders and, naturally, I made the squad.

I was so talented that I also made the squad once I got to Tougaloo College. I was also a part of the marching and concert bands in high school. Mr. Cole was a fantastic band teacher. I took physical education but did not play sports. My friend, Corine Hanshaw, and I very seldom ate in the cafeteria. We brought our lunches from home and during lunch time would either walk to her home to eat or go to my house at lunchtime. On the weekend, my other friends would get together and go to the movies on Sunday evenings and then to the colored drugstore (Mr. Dennis was the pharmacist). Afterward, we went back to BTU meetings at Union Baptist Church.

I was voted first runner-up to Miss Carver High in 1960. My friend, Ann Tyrus Pickett- Parker, was crowned queen and Eloise Bostic was next. Some things went down at that election that I question, but I let go and let God take care of it. My advice for students today regarding education is that it seems students today are all interested in instant gratification. We have made them, I would say, lazy. If education is prioritized as it was when I was in school, this current situation, especially among low-income families, can be turned around. The cure is to demand more from children and make education a priority. In the recent past, this seems to have started when school districts introduced school choice. As white parents left certain neighborhoods and schools, so did the tax base which supported those schools. Additionally, the parents and students who changed from previously all-black schools felt superior to the parents and students who stayed in predominantly black schools.

Parents these days share a big part of this situation because they don't want their children disciplined at school. They also do not discipline much at home either. This is the biggest contrast I experienced as a teacher compared to the rules my generation had at home about school, learning, and self-discipline. Our parents worked with and talked to teachers. Teachers came to our homes and discussed the grades we earned. Doing well in school was emphasized at home and connected to expectations for success in life later on. Unfortunately, too many parents today put more emphasis on what children are wearing instead of helping their children learn to read and write at home. There are still some ambitious children, however, who succeed in school and have risen above the system of welfare. It seems as if the more some parents give their children a vicious cycle sets in and too many children mimic the underachievement of their parents. If my parents could work and send twelve children to college *and* have all of them graduate, anything similar is possible.

6.   My name is **Valetta Thompson** and I am a 1960 graduate of Carver High School. My dear friend, Shirley (Barnes) Laird (on the right), is shown with me at an alumni function held some years ago. The subjects I studied during my school years were mathematics, English, history, science, music, library/study hall, and home economics. Some of the things I remember most about my school years were interacting with classmates, doing class assignments, and doing extracurricular activities. All of my teachers were memorable and played important roles in my quest to be an outstanding student. They were Mrs. V. P. Williams-Watts (science and mathematics), Mr. Marvin Pickett (history), Ms. Lou Ethel Gibson (English), Mrs. Towner (music), Mrs. Mattie Wallace Jennings (study hall/library) and Mrs. Luberta Seaborn (home economics).

During my time at Carver High School, I was a cheerleader for the football team, as well as a drum majorette in the band. The lasting friendship among my classmates is very meaningful to me. Attending Carver High School was a major stepping stone to my success on this journey called "life". The advice I have for today's youth is the same things I tell my grandchildren: keep God first, maintain good study habits, and read, read, read.

Valetta Thompson & Shirley Barnes

7. My name is **Edna Ruth Barnes** and I graduated from Carver High School in the Class of 1961. My years at Carver High School were the highlight of my teenage years. That is why I always look forward to our PN/CHS Reunion. I took the curriculum for each grade level 7-12. Some of the things I recall were eating in the lunchroom during special holidays, the football games at War Memorial Stadium, socials after the game at the recreation center, standing under the tree in front of the school after coming back from home at lunch, and going over to Thornhill's Grocery Store for my favorite… a snickers candy bar. Oh, the fun!!! I also enjoyed all my teachers even though I got a lot of detentions in the study hall because I love to talk. I was a cheerleader in high school but did not play sports. With regard to advice about the importance of education for today's youth, I offer the words of Mahatma Gandhi: "We must be the change we want to see". I have taught school since the mid-sixties and graduated from Jackson State University. My class recently celebrated

our Golden Anniversary (50ᵗʰ Year) as graduates of JSU. I believe I have modeled for my students (and myself) the change I want to see them achieve. Productive lives. You know … "talking the talk and walking the walk".

8.   My name is **Eddie Lee Titus** and I was in the Class of 1961 at Carver High School. My first school was St. Peter Catholic School and I was there for one year before I went to Pascagoula Negro Elementary School and then to Carver High …same campus. I studied math, history, English, science, and shop. My favorite classes were math, history, and shop. I had fun building furniture and getting blue ribbons during the Jackson County Fair. My favorite teachers were Mrs. Ernestine Fountain, Miss Gibson, and Miss V. P. Williams along with Mr. C. C. Boone, who was my football coach, and my math teacher. Later, I graduated from Oakland Tech High School in California.

When I played football at Carver High, I never came off the field. I was a running back, and defensive back, and I also returned punts and kickoffs. I have sent pictures of an award I received and a team picture. I am on the right (#27) and was Captain of our team with Co-captain R. L. Salter (#24, our quarterback). I cherish my days at Carver High and the many fun times with my friends and classmates. My dear friend, *Edna Ruth Barnes*, contacted me and told me about the CHS History Book project. I am part of Carver High and it will always be a part of me.

One other thing I would like to add is just a short story about life and living. I was offered a four-year scholarship to Cal Poly in San Luis Obispo. However, their football team's airplane crashed going in for a landing. Only six people survived. All were team players. John Madden and a team member named Major were survivors. John Madden later became the head coach of the Oakland Raiders and

SCHOOL DAYS 1948-49
ST. PETER

was afraid to fly but they had to fly because that was a part of his job. Major loved to fly. However, he refused to play football ever again. I met Major because his brother was one of my roommates at San Jose State. Major and I would always talk about all the cities we visited by flying. He never talked about football and I never asked why. I heard that Major passed away. When I think about Major, I wondered what he would say if I had told him that when I was coaching at the University of Santa Clara, the whole team faced death two times. The first time was flying to Northern California over the Pacific and #2 was flying to Canada. The plane had to turn back to Washington and we had to use another plane to Canada. I wish I could tell Major that story just to see what he would say when

I told him my choice is never to fly again. The university ended football in 1992. I have not been on a plane since. I think Major and I could have a good conversation. I received my BA in Sociology and Psychology and began a career as a probation officer. I later received a master's degree in political science while working as a probation officer. I retired after 41 years. I also coached the secondary at the University of Santa Clara from 1972 to 1992. I would often talk with the young men about getting a college education no matter how much.

9. My name is **Dorothy Richardson Harvey** and I graduated from Carver High School in the Class of 1963. During my high school years, I studied geometry, English (10th, 11th, and 12th grades), social studies, chemistry, and typing. Some of the things I remember most about my school years include the lifelong friends I made and the many teachers who pushed us to be our **very *best***. Although there was no gym, Union Baptist Church allowed us to have programs there. My favorite teacher was Mrs. V. P. Williams Watts and my favorite principal was Mr. B. B. Jennings, Sr. The only sport I remember during high school was football and we had very good teams. The head coach then was Mr. Aaron Jones. We did not have a lot of extracurricular activities but we had both band and choir. Both were very good, by my standards. I played 1st chair alto sax in the band under the direction of Mr. Edwin V. Cole. I also was the drum major in my senior year. In my senior year, our choir won 1st place at the state level under the direction of Mrs. Carolyn Bell Jennings.

My advice for today's youth regarding education is that education takes one a long way in life. One thing to remember is that "a journey of a thousand miles begins with a single step". Right now, completing high school is taking that single step. Work hard and care about others and your blessings will come in the form of a good productive life.

10. My name is **Odell L. Daniel** and I graduated in the Class of 1963 at Carver High School. I took all classes required for graduation. I played the coronet in the band but did not play sports. My favorite teacher was Ms. Gibson who taught me English. In later years, I went back to college at the age of 64. I studied theology at Our Lady of the Elms College and was later ordained a Roman Catholic Deacon. I currently serve at Holy Cross Roman Catholic Church in Springfield, MA. I am married and my wife is the director of Religious Education at Holy Cross Roman Catholic Church. We have a son living in Fl and a daughter who was called home by God. I also have two sisters and one brother whom I happily discovered through an Ancestry. com search. My advice to the youth of today

is to get your education. It unlocks a world of possibilities and a better life. To get ordained, I worked the night shift and drove 25-30 miles to school the next day for three years until I got my theological education. Get your education and *never give up*.

11. My name is **Carolyn Sue Barnes McCain** and I am a 1964 graduate of Carver High School. During my school years, the courses I studied were part of our basic curriculum. Mathematics (algebra I/II), general math, science (general science, chemistry, and biology), world history, social studies, U. S. history, music, and band. What I remember most about my school years is that school was not a place to play around. My teachers were quite thorough with all of the information we were given. They were serious about the learning process and there were few if any, behavior problems in all of my classes. Students came to class to learn. I had some very good teachers and there was no playing around in class. We kept the learning process going and we also helped each other. I had some very good teachers at Carver High School. Mr. Aaron Jones, and Mrs. V. P. Williams-Watts (taught me algebra I and II). Mr. B. B. Jennings, Sr. was my principal. His son, Mr. B. B. Jennings, Jr., taught me biology. He nicknamed the females in class "the nurses". Miss Gibson and Mr. Moore were my English teachers. They were great teachers. Miss Lola Bell was my homeroom and typing teacher. Additionally, all of my teachers emphasized internalizing good ethics.

My advice to the students of today is to be the best student they can be. Learning in school is a continuous, yearly cycle with more to learn in each subject. Be serious about the learning process and be enthusiastic about learning. Have a plan for your future and be able to adjust to circumstances life throws your way. Doing so will help you to more easily adjust to the demands of our changing society.

12. My name is **Norma Jean Larkins Jackson**. I graduated from Carver High School in 1964. I retired from Ingalls as a secretary and later as an apprentice program counselor. During my high school years, I studied English, math (algebra I/II), home economics, history (American and World), Shop, and typing. For about six weeks Mr. Taylor taught girls shop and Mrs. Lucas taught boys home economics. My husband, **Charles Jackson** (Class of 1963), did not take home economics. I think offering the optional classes in this way was done because the teachers and principal thought boys needed to learn how to cook, etc., and girls needed to learn how to make certain things with wood. Charles took the required courses and Shop. He learned brickwork and carpentry which came in handy around his house. Charles also played football. I loved the CHS tradition of giving your favorite player an apple

after the game…win or lose. He remembers a game we lost to Picayune. The team later took it out on Waynesboro, beating them 93-0. Charles indicated that his favorite teachers were Miss Gibson (English) and Mr. Pickett (History). Charles has retired after 42 years as a tugboat engineer at Colle Towing Company.

I played clarinet in the band and later the oboe. I enjoyed marching and performing in the band and we often won marching and concert season band competitions. Miss V. P. (math) was my favorite teacher along with Miss Lola Bell who taught me typing. Her class helped me to get a job at Ingalls. I worked there as a secretary for 36 years.

I also want to mention the work our PTA did to help get us band uniforms. I modeled the first new uniform we got during a PTA meeting. Before then we wore white shirts, black pants, and white tennis shoes. I recall that my favorite class was algebra taught by Miss V. P. Williams and home economics taught by Mrs. Lucas. I loved both classes. I credit Mrs. Lucas for helping me to learn how to sew. Later in life, I made Patricia Stallworth Hanshaw's wedding gown with the help of my aunt, Mrs. Marguerite Hanshaw. After that, I made my daughter's wedding gown by myself and taught her to sew. I became so good that I also made clothes for myself and my sisters. Neighborhood girls benefitted as well because they learned to sew aprons and skirts at my home.

Charles Jackson, Class of 1963

A big influence on my life is the diploma my mother received in 1937. She encouraged us to complete high school and get as much education as we could. I treasure the high school diploma she earned and gave to me. It is included with our statement and hangs on the wall in our home. The advice Charles and I give to the students of today is that they must pay special attention to instructions from their teachers. It is so important.

Be serious about learning and what career you might want to pursue. Start that process early but be especially focused on your career/dreams once in high school.

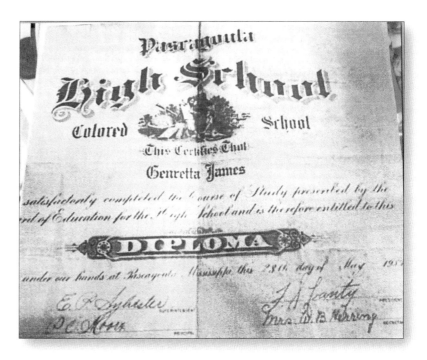

High School Diploma of Mrs. Genretta James, 1937. P. C. Moore, Principal

Take advantage of apprentice programs because I worked in that area at Ingalls. Apprenticeship programs are available in other industries as well as local hospitals. I know of several people who got their start in apprenticeship programs and have done well in life.

It is also important to have God in your life. A number of my classmates belonged to various churches and faiths. We still agreed on the value of having a spiritual influence in your life. Such an influence can help you balance the hard times and disappointments with the joy of overcoming setbacks and achieving one's goals and dreams. We just have to play our part and not be discouraged by disappointments. Nothing beats a failure but a try. Never stop trying.

Lastly, Charles and I recommend that all parents send their kids to kindergarten. It can be a wonderful learning experience. They can get, as I did, an early start learning how to read and write. This exposure may benefit the children of parents who choose to send their children to kindergarten before beginning elementary school.

13. My name is **Sandra Burton Barnes** and I am a graduate of Carver High School, Class of 1965. I took courses in English, history, world history, Mississippi history, and civics. I also took typing, and shorthand along with home economics, math, and biology. I enjoyed playing the flute in the band and singing in the school choir. Some of the things I remember most is how the whole community

supported us. Teachers, parents, the community, churches, and businesses all contributed to our education. They made hot dogs, sold fish sandwiches, made candy, and sold hot cocoa at football games which helped us to have snacks at football games. These sorts of fundraisers also helped to buy/replace mouthpieces and reeds for band members who may not have been able to purchase their own. Some of the teachers also belonged to the same churches and organizations. They knew us and wanted us to succeed.

My favorite teacher was Ms. Gibson (English). She demanded that students spoke correct English. I remember congregating verbs, diagramming sentences, and identifying and/or distinguishing between nouns, pronouns, and adverbs. I wonder when I hear people speaking nowadays if schools still teach English. A prominent joke in school was when someone would say "where you at?", the response would be behind the preposition. I loved Ms. Gibson's style. She was always dressed so neatly. Her high-heeled shoes, sharp outfits, and how she presented herself impressed me as a young teenager. Her class made English my favorite subject. I simply wanted to be like her. I also liked history. I remember Mr. Marvin Pickett's teaching of Mississippi History because we learned the state song and often sang "Way Down South in Mississippi". I still remember some of the lines ("…food so good and the future so bright"). Sports was not a part of my school experience. However, I was in the band under the direction of Mr. Cole. As I mentioned earlier, I played the flute and I still have it to this day. I will always remember one football game when Carver High played against Mattie Blunt from Mobile, AL. During the halftime show, the visiting band performed first. They had two drum majorettes twirling their batons and strutting their stuff as the high-stepping band played "Hit the Road Jack by Ray Charles. Their band was rocking and the stadium crowd was going wild. We had to follow that! In those days, we had been taught standard marching band songs and formations. We performed songs by John Phillip Sousa and I must admit it was a little boring but also educational (i.e., Stars and Stripes Forever, Seventy-six Trombones, to name a few). However, we pulled ourselves together and did what we practiced even though it was, by comparison, "nothing nice". Some 58 years later, I still remember that. I also would like to add that we won a trophy as the *Best High School Choir* in the State of Mississippi under the direction of Ms. Carolyn (Bell) Jennings, our Choir Director. Mr. Pickett and Mr. Moore were also a part of the team. To win the championship, we sang acapella a Negro spiritual "Little Lamb, Little Lamb, I'm gonna serve God till I die". The competition was held at Jackson State University in Jackson, MS.

Sandra Burton Barnes, Former PN/CHSAA President

The advice that I have for today's youth regarding education is to take your education very, very, seriously. You are preparing for your future and life moves fast. Show respect for yourselves, your teachers, and your elders. And if by chance you stumble along the way, forgive yourselves. Learn lessons from your mistakes and keep trying. Stay positive because there's light at the end of the tunnel.

14. My name is **Pastor ONeil Wiley** and I graduated Salutatorian in the Class of 1965 at Carver High School. I am the Presiding Elder of the Jefferson District of West Alabama Conference of the AME Zion Church and Pastor of AME Zion Church in Pascagoula, MS. My favorite subjects were math, science (biology and chemistry), and English. My favorite teachers were Ms. Gibson, Ms. V. P. Williams, Mr. Pickett, and Mr. Knight. Principal Jennings was one of my favorites as well. Some of the things I remember most were science fair competitions and traveling to compete in high school football. I played quarterback. I also recall eating good food in the cafeteria and presiding as President of my senior class. I enjoyed all of my high school years and have nothing but fond memories.

My advice to the youth of today about education is that they should learn as much as possible by taking advantage of every learning experience. Additionally, have a solid moral and spiritual foundation. Get as much education as possible while you are young. Put aside anything that might be a distraction or hindrance. Set specific goals and persevere until you achieve them. Make education a lifelong lifestyle.

15. My name is **Roland Charles Fisher**. I am a graduate of Carver High School in the Class of 1965. My favorite subjects were math, English, typing, and biology. The most memorable times I recall involved

Roland C. Fisher, Air Traffic Controller

my transition from a Catholic school environment to a public school environment. In my early youth, I was balancing school and a career as a butcher and cashier in two neighborhood grocery stores on the north side of Pascagoula (i.e., Midway Grocery and Wayne Lee's Grocery). They were staples in communities near north Market for many of my schoolmates during my four years at Carver. Wayne Lee's today is still a key business in neighborhoods even across city boundaries.

My favorite teachers were Mr. Taylor and Ms. Lou Ethel Gibson. I took typing from Ms. Bell. Coincidentally, she replaced Ms. Lola Bell who also taught typing for many years before I came to Carver. My favorite principal was Mr. Johnson. I was never involved in sports. However, singing in the choir and mastering typing were my favorites during my junior and senior years. The educational and life skills learned at Carver High school provided me with the foundation to become a 45-year military professional. I have

mastered skills as an Air Traffic Controller, educator, professional career counselor, and IT Specialist with over 35 certifications. Ms. Belle's typing class in 1964 paid off throughout my journey.

I would like to pass on a few thoughts to our youth of today. Start preparing for your future today. Learn as much as you can from teachers, family, church members, and neighbors about their achievements. Ask for help with subjects that appear to be hurdles. Learn from those part-time jobs whether they pay a lot or not. Those life skills are free and sometimes not taught in school. Make certain your career goals match your employment goals and always maintain your faith.

The Legend Has Retired

16. My name is **Larry G. Hanshaw, Ph.D.,** and I graduated as Valedictorian in the Class of 1965 at Carver High School. I studied math (algebra I/II with trigonometry), geometry, civics, general math, English I-IV, U. S. history, biology, chemistry, and typing. Mr. Aaron Jones, during our civics class, took us to see how the criminal justice system worked by visiting the courtroom of Judge Watts. He also encouraged us to look to the future when he took our seventh-grade class on a bus trip to Jackson State. For the trip, my classmates attached a huge sign to our school bus "*Seventh Grade Future Seekers*". I liked all of my teachers but Mr. Pickett, Mr. Moore, Mrs. V. P. Williams-Watts, Mr. Cole, Mr. Knight, Mr. Taylor, and Mr. B. B. Jennings (biology teacher) equally stand out for different reasons. Through their leadership styles, Principals Jennings, Duckworth, and Johnson helped me to understand how difficult it was to manage our high school's needs in an environment where others too often had the final say. Some other things I recall were playing trumpet in the band from sixth grade to twelfth and singing in talent shows. Eugene Brown, Ora Stewart, Richard Patton, Willie Davis, and I won first place singing, acapella, "*A Mexican Divorce*" [by The Drifters]. I sang the tenor lead. Two other memories stand out from my high school years. The first is my mother's decision not to sign the permission form to let me play football (quarterback) even though Mr. Jones and Mr. Knight came by twice trying to change her mind. She told them that "someone is going to play that trumpet I paid $150 for". She then turned and looked directly at me. There was no further discussion. The blessing in disguise was the fact that my band grades (all As since sixth grade), played a decisive role in my having the highest grade-point average in my senior class. For that and many other reasons, I am thankful for my mother's wisdom.

Parents often see in their children what children may not see in themselves. I am certain I am not the only one. I am including a picture of my *mother's high school diploma* as valedictorian of her class in May 1938. Thomas Wells was Superintendent and P. C. Moore was the Principal at *Pascagoula High School Colored School*. Thanks for your guidance, mama.

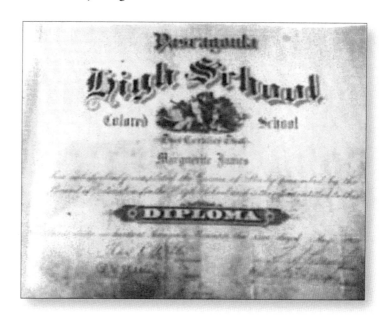

The second memory that stands out happened in 1960 at a district band competition at Oak Park High School in Laurel, MS. Our band was boarding the bus when my sister, Corine, asked me to get her a coke. Mr. Cole gave his O.K. and Robert Campbell, another trumpet player, and I went to the coke and vending machines to get some snacks. As we were getting snacks, a group of 4-5 Oak Park High band members stopped us; one with a knife drawn and held near my face and throat area. They determined that I was not the person they were looking for after one of the Oak Park band members said "No, he's not the one". They left and we reported what happened to Mr. Cole. Years later, during my freshman year at Tougaloo College, I reminded my then-college classmate of the incident at his high school. His actions (and God's blessings) saved me from potential injury or even being killed. I recently saw him and other classmates at the funeral of another college classmate, Supervisor Melton Harris. We remain friends.

My advice to today's youth regarding education is that they should stay in school every year until they graduate. Take the subjects needed to support the major that must be declared when they get to college. Check out the helpful information in the *Occupational Outlook Handbook* at the local library or one's high school or a nearby college or university. It can answer important questions about courses needed relative to planned careers. Take courses online to get a degree or trade school certification. Lastly, apply for a Wall of Fame (WOF) scholarship and become an Heir supporter of the PN/CHS Alumni Association, Inc.

17. My name is **Cecil A. Paris** and I graduated from Carver High School in the Class of 1966. In high school, I concentrated on the sciences and math. Specifically, I liked life science, chemistry, and algebra. Overall, the subject matter was limited. There were no advanced courses beyond first-year

Cecil Paris

chemistry and second-semester algebra. However, teachers made an extra effort to support interested students by encouraging participation in district and state science fairs. The student enrollment, compared to other schools, was small. Therefore, the association with other students was close. Everyone at least knew the names of other students since the daily contact was limited to one building.

My favorite teacher is a difficult subject because all of my teachers supported my efforts and encouraged extracurricular activities. Mr. Marvin Pickett was my favorite as a homeroom teacher. He took a profound interest in non-academic accomplishments as well. Miss V. P. Williams and coach James Smith were my favorite science and mathematics teachers. They had a thorough knowledge of the subject matter and made it interesting. Mr. B. B. Jennings was the same with biology, which otherwise would have been an uninteresting subject. I played football (i.e., quarterback). I was on my way to being an outstanding performer (I think), and my coaches felt the same way. This was cut short because I finished early after the 11th grade. I was designated to be the number one quarterback for my senior year. I played in the marching band (i.e., tuba). I loved the concert season as well. I received several awards for two solo renditions at district and state band festivals. Concert music was responsible for my developing an appreciation for a broad spectrum of composers. This background enabled me to earn a music scholarship during my senior year at Tuskegee Institute. This was the first year Tuskegee offered scholarships in sports and music participation. This opportunity for financial support all began with handed-down instruments while at Carver High School.

Carver High was a small school in a small coastal town. We had very limited resources compared to other schools. No gymnasium to encourage and develop indoor sports, no advanced academic courses beyond second-semester algebra, and no physics, calculus, automotive mechanics, or intermediate-level vocational studies. In most instances, we used outdated textbooks. Despite all of these shortcomings and handicaps, we were still able to produce some outstanding students able to compete on a national level and able to achieve above-average scores on college entrance exams. I attribute this to the dedication of teachers who considered their positions as a profession and not just a job. To students who loved competition and supported and encouraged each other to make the best effort within them to achieve their goals, our teachers were there to support us. This was called *Hornet Pride*. Something that could not be bought or donated. It is something that is instilled. At Carver High, it was an ongoing action.

My advice to today's youth is in the context of living in a highly technical society. Each year, dozens of new terms are created to describe a new operation or routine function. Education and learning are necessary and basic components of living. The academic and industrial diversity of this country has created a shortage of specialized/experienced individuals needed to fulfill the growing demand for needed talent. I would encourage all youth to take that *good old Carver High pride* and pursue studies either academically or vocationally and treat themselves to an increased standard of living rather than mere survival.

18. My name is **William Holmes** and I am a graduate of Carver High School in the Class of 1966. I took all of the courses required for graduation. I did not play in the band but I did play football (#64). In relation to football, I also engaged in bodybuilding. This choice helped me personally because it made me better at sports and it improved my health. I liked all of my teachers, coaches, and principals.

I also made lasting friendships as a student at Carver High. I also combined principles learned as a member of the Boy Scouts of America ("…keep myself physically strong, mentally awake, and morally straight…") with school and sports. This combination made me a better person. In 1962, I was one of the first boy scouts to go to Philmont Scout Ranch in Cimarron, New Mexico as a Life Scout. After returning home, I became an Eagle Scout. I was employed at Ingalls Shipbuilding until 1973 and retired from Chevron in 1999 after 26 years as a pipefitter, pipe welder, and crane operator. I opened Community Cleaners in 2011 and my wife, Julia F. Rodgers Holmes (Class of 1968), and I ran a successful business for many years. I have included a couple of photographs with my statement.

My advice to young people today is to get an education (i.e., high school, community college, four-year college degree, or trade school certification) and apply it to today's challenges. Along with working hard, you also might achieve your dreams. Whether it is football, school, weightlifting, or scouting, be the best person you can be. Along the way in life, you might become the person who will inspire someone else to achieve their goals and dreams. I look forward to reading the contributions of others in the upcoming History of Carver High School.

19. My name is **Virginia Russell Jackson Richard** and I graduated in the Class of 1967. In high school, I took math, science, history, home economics (under Mrs. Lucas), English, and biology. Our teachers were very supportive and wanted us to further our education. They talked to students to help them prepare for life. My favorite teacher in biology was Mr. B. B. Jennings and Miss Lou Ethel Gibson in English. Mr. B. B. Jennings, Sr. was my favorite Principal. I did not play sports but did play the bells in the band. I got help learning to play the bells from Carolyn Cunningham and, in return, when I moved to first chair, I helped Alfredia Colston learn to play the bells. We often put down our bells and started dancing as our band played certain songs. My high school experiences were some of the best years anyone could ask for. I felt prepared when I went to Jackson State interacting with students from other cities who had different life experiences. The advice I would give to youth is "if at first, you don't succeed, try and try again". The world is an open library that teaches good and bad lessons.

20. My name is **Diane J. Barnes** and I graduated from Carver High School in the Class of 1967 During my high school years, I took English, social studies, home economics, math, and PE. My favorite subject was physical education and my favorite teacher was Miss Ida Massey. She wore starched and ironed PE uniforms to school. It made me Interested in physical education. She was very detailed and once I became a teacher, I modeled myself after her. I played in the band and sang in the choir under Ms. Carolyn Bell. We won choir championships on the coast and in Jackson. My favorite principal was Mr. Jennings. He also cut my dad's hair on the weekends. My other favorite teacher was Ms. Lou Ethel Gibson. Miss Gibson taught vocabulary building in her English class. We had to define words from the dictionary and use the words appropriately in sentences. Once I got to JSU, the assignments in my English class under Drs. D. Kincaid Robinson and Cyphus Smith were the same as the assignments I did in Ms. Gibson's English class. I was taught well at Carver High School. As a 4H Club member, I was very active and traveled a lot. "Head, Heart, Hand, and Health" was our motto. I learned a lot about cooking while in 4H and this helped later in life and at home. 4H also connected well with home economics taught by Ms. Lucas. For years, I kept the potholders and apron I made in 4H which, by the way, won Honorable Mention. I also was one of the students who participated in taking shop under Mr. Taylor. Some males in my class took home economics under Ms. Lucas. This was quite an

experience because I learned how wood is used to make useful things just as certain boys learned how to cook certain meals from scratch.

My advice to students of today is I strongly suggest that students carefully listen to what teachers have to say. Likewise, teachers should spend more time talking to students one-on-one. The result may be that teachers can help a child deal with issues that arise and learn from students what their problems might be. Talking to students is one way to reach out and, perhaps, change a student's life.

21. My name is **Glenn Thomas Larkins** and I graduated from Carver High School in 1967. Some of the courses I took were English, social studies, math, shop, and science. My favorite teacher was Ms. Gibson who taught English and helped me a lot. Throughout my life, I have dealt with stuttering. It creates a false image of a person and she understood this more than others. Principal Johnson and Coach Jones were also favorites of mine. Billy Knight was my basketball and running back coach who was

also encouraging. Some of the things I recall about my high school years were playing football and basketball. I was a running back on the football team, very fast, and I could catch the ball. We beat Magnolia High School when I played. I scored in every game against them. We tied for the Gulf Coast Championship in my senior year. After I graduated from Carver High, Morris Richardson (Spaceman) and I went to Perkinston Junior College where we played football but I also ran track. In 1967, Morris Richardson (below with his wife) and I won numerous trophies and were the first African American members of Perkinston Junior College's football team. I set records in track at Perk which *have not been broken to this day.* I invite everyone to visit the campus and see the many trophies Morris and I won in track and football. I also attended Tennessee State University for 1.5 years where I was known as "the blur". I later returned home and worked as a foreman for the City of Pascagoula's Sewer Department. I retired after about 40 years of employment. Recently, the Pascagoula Athletic Foundation honored Morris and me for our athletic achievements. I have included two photographs showing the gold

medallions and trophies we received. My advice to young people is to stay in school and graduate. Life is much easier with an education.

The picnics, Motown Showdown, and Draw Down are my favorites because such events provide scholarships for the next generation. I know Morris, another WOF member, feels the same way.

22. My mane is **Dr. Donald Wright** and I graduated in the Class of 1967. During my high school years, I took history, science, government (civics), and geography. My favorite subject was history. My favorite teacher was the late Ms. Geraldine Barnes. I remember most ideas about how to become a leader and how to present yourself professionally. My teachers and high school counselor helped me to understand these concepts.

Sports were a part of my high school experience. Football, basketball, and baseball were my favorites. The more I learned, I shared with other students who sought my counsel. My advice to students regarding education is that they should love the Lord and pray mightily. Always seek God first in everything. I am currently Deacon Emeritus in my church and believe that if we can spread love as quickly as we spread hate and negativity, an amazing and better world is what we would live in. To God be the glory.

23. My name is **Andrew Jackie Elly**. I graduated from Carver High School in the Class of 1967. My wife, Faye, and I are parents of four boys, one girl, and 16 grandchildren. My favorite subject in school was history taught by Mr. Aaron Jones. I enjoyed all of my classes and teachers because they contributed to my success at Carver High and later in college. My experiences at Carver made me even more determined to do the right things to be successful no matter the challenge. Other things I

remember most about my time at Carver High were the football games and the close relationships between our students. I especially enjoyed the band even though I never played in the band. The performances of our drum majors were entertaining because they put on a good show every Saturday night. We played our games on Saturday nights because the white schools played on Friday nights. We usually got old uniforms for the sports offered at Carver High. They were passed down to us after they were used at the white high school across town. In all of my years at Carver, I don't remember anything ever getting out of hand. We had a lot of respect for one another. Our teachers demanded that we focus on going to college as a choice for a successful life. Everybody got along then and continues to have great friendships now. I also would like to share with you the school experiences and challenges to be our best by Coach Jones, Coach Knight, and Coach McIntyre. They did not just pass us because we played sports. We had to earn our grades.

In 1965, our gym was built. It is now the Aaron Jones family interactive center. It benefits kids in our community in a variety of ways. We never had really good basketball teams until after I left. In football, I looked up to a lot of players. I remember Calvin Huey, Joe Tyrus, George Paris, Brady Walker, and Robert Martin. They were people who went to various colleges and came back to talk with us and with Coach Jones. I also recall that the choir was a real go- getter and won a state championship under Ms. Carolyn Bell. The choir, led by Mr. Pickett and Mr. Moore woke up the crowd whenever our Alma Mater was sung by the choir. It is still sung with a lot of energy and heart right now. Carver always competed in the top 10% in competitions. Before Carver High School, however, I started at St. Peter Catholic School up to the 8th grade. We were well prepared there and learned that our color was natural and good and to be proud of who we are. Out of the top ten in my class at Carver High, six of the top 10 graduates were males and that is something you don't see a lot of today. I remember Dr. Hanshaw, George Paris, Johnny Magee, and others. I remember those gentlemen because of how smart they were. I also remember Frank Miller as a good student and a very good football player. At Carver High, you were either in the band, played football, or were in the choir. Regardless, the guys in either activity pushed us to be the best we could be. I graduated in the top 10% of my class at CHS.

The advice I have for today's youth regarding education is that they should evaluate everything that they do and try to be productive citizens. They should avoid getting into trouble. They also should be their own person. Try to get the best education whether it is a trade of interest or a college education. Opportunities are out there for people who want to be successful in life. Don't allow society or the system to dictate your future. Dictate your own. Stay away from drugs. By doing so you will likely find that your future is in your hands and not in the hands of someone else.

24. My name is **Brenda Miller Johnson**, **Attorney-at-Law**, and I am a graduate of Carver High School in the Class of 1968. After the murder of Emmitt Till, my father moved his family to Pascagoula from Inverness, MS in 1955. He preferred a job on the coast instead of becoming an overseer for a cotton plantation owner in Inverness. Hornet members of my family who also graduated from Carver High are (1) George Miller, Class of 1959, a retired U. S. Army veteran who also played football and was in the band, was a U.S. Army veteran, retired police lieutenant, and WOF member; (2) Juliareen Miller (Williams), Class of 1960, played basketball, was in the band, choir, and wrote beautiful poetry; and (3) Frank Miller, an awesome defensive tackle who starred in football at CHS and played with Depriest Randall and Elliott Jackson. Frank also was a star in the same position at Mississippi Valley State with teammate and (fellow CHS Hornet) Harold Pleasant and others.

*Atty. Brenda Miller Johnson, CHS Wall of Fame
and First WOF Committee Chairperson*

Two of my elementary school teachers stand out. Ms. Whitehead let me "take names" whenever she left the room and Mrs. Chapman taught me about germs. Her discussions helped me since then to deal with my fear of germs. At Carver High, I looked up to upperclassmen (but I half-feared and half-admired Roland fisher and James Howard Evans). One of my favorite teachers was Ms. Lou Ethel

Gibson. In her English class, students were encouraged to read short stories, poetry, and read books brought to our school by the Book Mobile. She assigned me "Catcher in the Rye" (J. D. Salinger) to read and make a book report. I completed the assignment and then she asked me to present my report to several other classes. She once submitted one of my original stories to a publishing company. These are examples of how teachers at Carver High cared about, inspired, and boosted our confidence. She made me believe in myself. A little more about Ms. Gibson later.

I was co-captain of the basketball team and played with Eva Stallworth, Elaine Durden, Julia Campbell, Carolyn Stennis, Sharon Patton, Lizzie Mae Goldsmith, and others. I wore jersey number 32. I was passionate about basketball. However, the first time I tried out for the team, I didn't make it. After I got coaching from William "Papa Hayes", I made the team. In one tournament, I was tossed out of the game by the referee for judo-chopping an opposing player. I suppose my passion got a little out of hand. Led by my neighbor, Shirley Williams, I learned cheerleading skills and became captain during football season joined by my dear friend, Shirley Willis.

After several jobs, I got my dream job at Ingalls Ship Building Corporation en route to pursuing my ultimate goal of going to college. Mrs. V. P. Williams-Watts along with others at Carver High and, particularly, the Class of 1969, helped me realize it is "never too late" to get on the right track even after making a non-traditional personal decision. I finally made up my mind to go to college. I resigned from Ingalls on a Friday and was at Jackson State College (now JSU) the following Monday morning. I embellished my situation a bit with the admissions office and after a few hours, I was admitted.

With little or no funds, I needed a job to help pay my college expenses. My answer was to study harder and pray even harder. With help from Dr. Jefferson, an English professor at JSU, I got a job after he asked me who my English teacher was in high school. When he learned it was Ms. Lou Ethel Gibson, I got a job tutoring. This connection to my Carver High story is what I alluded to earlier. I finished at JSU in 1972 with a major in Speech/Communication and a minor in Psychology. I also got a job from Dr. Rose McCoy which allowed me to finish my degree in 1972. I returned to the coast and taught at Magnolia in Moss Point. I also applied for that technical writing job at Ingalls which I was told years earlier required at least 2 years of experience. Then, I was deemed underqualified. This time around, however, I was told I was "overqualified" by the Personnel Manager at Ingalls. True story.

I worked in the federal sector for 30 years before retiring. I am now in my *second career* as an attorney which I began shortly before retiring. I earned my Juris Doctorate at Miles Law School in Birmingham, was elected Student Bar Association President, and graduated Salutatorian in my class. I have practiced law for 20 years. My advice to the youth of today regarding education is this: Be confident. Set realistic goals. Explore avenues for scholarships and financial aid. Keep the faith and give back. No matter the situation, get up and go until you reach your goal because it is *never too late*.

25. My name is **Wanda Bonita Barnes Hanshaw** and I am a graduate of Carver High School in the Class of 1968. In high school, I studied English, math, science (biology), general science, history, world history, and music (band). I played the clarinet. I also enjoyed traveling to band concerts and playing in the marching band at football games and performing in hometown parades. I didn't have

a favorite teacher but I liked all of them. I learned a lot at Carver High School. Somewhere along the way, I developed a love for art and loved to draw. I studied hard in school in all of my classes, but on one occasion, I got up to say my speech in Ms. Gibson's English class and drew a blank. You might say that experience underlined the meaning of empathy as a quality any good teacher must have. I never forgot the second chance I got to do better.

During the time I lived in Virginia, I earned a master's degree in Special Education at the College of William & Mary. I enjoyed educating students with special needs and later taught at Vancleave High School for over 25 years. After I retired, I worked at MS Gulf Coast Community College in Gulfport During giving GED tests to students who were trying to improve their educational background. My teachers at CHS were often on my mind as I encountered students who needed encouragement to improve their chances in life.

Maybe it was fate, but Larry Hanshaw's Sunday School teacher, and one of his Explorer Scout Troop Leaders, was my father, Ephram Barnes. He and Mr. Leroy Russell took scouts to Keesler Air force Base to see the Blue Angels and Thunderbirds. The scouts also learned about military life in relation to scouting. We trade stories about my father all the time. Larry's Explorer Scout badge, earned at Keesler Air Force Base, is in a frame and hangs in his office to this day.

I am very fond of *Mrs. Rhenetta Blake* (next page)who taught me in elementary school. We laughed and talked about old times and enjoyed each other's memories during her husband's interview for the CHS History Book. Following Mr. Blake's photo, I also have included a family photograph. I am *in the middle* with my hand on my father's shoulder. He used to say: "No matter if the job is large or small, do it well or not at all". It is interesting how sayings learned in one's youth tend to stick like glue in your memory. In turn, such words of wisdom and encouragement were used by me throughout my teaching career and lifetime. I am the twelfth in a family of twelve. Some of my brothers and sisters are also featured/remembered in this history book. All of them graduated from CHS except Ms. Geraldine Barnes. She graduated from Prentiss Institute during her high school years. Our family put education right behind serving the Lord. Like many other families, we took both related teachings to heart and worked hard to help each other be successful. My mother and father worked hard to make us who we are. My sisters Maxine and Eloise are not in the family photograph. The men in my family did their part to help out as well. In the same family photo, they are from left to right: Dr. Lionel Barnes, Glennis Earl (Nick) Barnes, and C. B. Barnes. I love and dearly miss all of my brothers and sisters, but especially those whom God has called to rest.

*From L: Wanda Hanshaw, Mrs. Rhenetta
Blake, and Mr. Johnny Blake*

The History of Carver High School: 1890 – 1970   **95**

Barnes Family photo

The advice I offer to today's youth is from my own life experiences and lessons learned at home. Attend school until you graduate. Study hard and complete all assignments because doing so will improve your chances in life.

Be prayerful about any problems in your life and go to church to learn about God for yourself. Register to vote and use this power to elect people who will follow the U. S. Constitution no matter the state in which you reside. My parents believed in voting. It is important to make your wishes known. Finally, be proud of and support our Hornet Nation at Carver High School.

26. My name is **Julia Rodgers-Holmes** and I am a 1968 graduate of Carver High School in Pascagoula, MS. I am shown below with my husband, **William**, who graduated in the Class of 1966. From grades nine through 12, I followed the college preparatory path which included geometry, biology, chemistry, algebra, and physics. Our class was the first to be taught physics by Mr. Preston Graves in our senior year. Our teachers were able to get their master's degrees paid for by International Paper and they took advantage of this great opportunity.

We rarely had new textbooks. The books, typewriters, and other equipment were often hand-me-downs from the local white junior high and high school. Despite this unequal playing field, our teachers went beyond the call of duty. They worked hard to give us a well-rounded education. I remember

working hard in every class, working hard at home, and participating in activities at my church. This carried over to my job. I found time to hang out with my friends at the "rec", Miller's Dairy bar, football games, and basketball games. Sometimes, we would sneak off to Biloxi to go to the Shalamar. At school, I participated in the student council, Tri-Hi-Y, 4H Club, and choir. I fondly remember wiener roasts and hayrides. Although I didn't play organized sports, we played all kinds of sports in the street with our family and friends. Most of us knew how to dance, roller skate, and swim. I cannot say I had a favorite teacher or principal because I truly loved and benefitted from each of them. To this day, I have a good rapport and deep respect for Mayor Billy Knight, Mr. and Mrs. B. B. Jennings, Mr. Marvin Pickett, Mr. Richard Moore, Mr. James McIntyre, Mrs. Hilda Walton Bragg, and Mr. James Winters. The principals I had were Mr. C. J. Duckworth, Mr. Louis Peyton, and Mr. Willie Johnson. They were very effective leaders.

During the summer of 1964, I attended Freedom School on DuPont Ave. My teacher was Marionne Ingram, author of **Hands of War and Hands of Peace**. We also met Bob Moses, Hosea Williams, John Lewis, and several other famous civil rights activists. They were amazed at how well we were able to read and excel in practically everything that they put before us. Well, I attribute all of that to my dedicated elementary school Principal Mrs. Ernestine Fountain, and my second-grade teacher Mrs. Bernie Sowell. Both bought me books because I had read almost all the library books on the Bookmobile.

Mrs. Mattie Woods Jennings, our librarian, and Mayor Billy Knight, my homeroom teacher and algebra teacher, profoundly affected my life. After attending Freedom School and meeting Marionne, I was inspired to read even more. After freedom summer, Mrs. Jennings let me work in the school library until my senior year. The following year, Mr. Knight and Mr. J. B. Carter, who ran Neighborhood Youth Corp, ask Mrs. Kathleen McIlwain if I could work in the Pascagoula library. She agreed and I worked there for four years instead of summers only. As a result, I became the first black person to work in the Jackson-George County Regional Library System. My best advice for students is to try hard to research their future careers. With college costs soaring, I would suggest students ask school counselors or trusted educators to help them determine what courses or experiences will best enable them to attend a trade school or college. Students may find that a trade school is a better choice. Between these options, trade schools cost much less than a traditional four-year college education. Also, jobs in the trades are booming while other job opportunities are oversaturated by four-year applicants.

27. My name is **Judy R. Coffey** and I graduated in the Class of 1968 at Carver High School. During my school years, I studied the general courses offered as well as the college prep curriculum. I worked hard in all of my classes. I especially enjoyed the camaraderie exhibited among all students. My first-grade teacher, Mrs. Hicks, was my favorite. My favorite subject in high school was history. I

did not play organized sports. However, I was a part of the high school marching band and the concert band. Both were enjoyable and provided opportunities to meet students at other schools and, in some cases, make new friends. I also would like to add that because of my teachers and counselors who took a genuine interest in me, their efforts helped mold me into the person I am today.

I am a graduate of Jackson State University and recently celebrated my 50th Anniversary Graduation. I have retired from the field of Social Work and enjoy attending sports events, working at my local church, traveling, and returning home for our high school alumni activities. Decorating our class float, participating in talent show activities, and seeing classmates and friends have been rewarding experiences over the years. The advice that I offer to today's youth regarding education is that they should take their education seriously. Moreover, they should get to know their teachers and other students. One can never tell when you may be able to provide assistance to someone else or receive the help you might need from someone else. Either way, you will be enriched and will grow in a variety of ways. Be prayerful throughout life and remember that it is certainly true that a "mind is a terrible thing to waste".

28. My name is **Brenda F. Stallworth Dread**. I graduated from Carver High School in 1969. I am married to Orzie L. Dread, Jr. We are the proud parents of two loving daughters and two beautiful grandchildren. During my school years, I took English, math, science, history, physical education, home economics, and typing. My favorite teachers were Mrs. Mattie Woods Jennings and Mr. Alexander. I enjoyed my years at Carver High School. I had great educators and they encouraged us to learn. However, my first educators were my parents. They instilled in me the desire to learn so that I could have a better life than they did.

My advice to today's youth regarding education is to finish school. In addition, they should love, honor, obey, and respect their teachers and elders. I would tell the youth of today that they have a privilege our forefathers never experienced. There is financial help available to earn an education. They must choose to use productively the great minds that our Lord gave them.

29. My name is **Patricia Ann Stallworth Hanshaw**. I graduated in the Class of 1970 as the Salutatorian of my class. I met my soul mate, Michael A. Hanshaw, at Carver High School, married him in later years, and created a loving family with four loving children. During my school years, I studied English, History, Economics, Science, Algebra l and ll, Geometry,

Physical Education/Health, Biology, and Typing. Some of the things I remember most about my school years were the sunny days I walked across town to school with my sisters and brothers. On rainy days, we rode to school in my uncle John Sabino's car with my cousins. My school days and school years were structured and the teachers created a safe learning environment. Another fond memory is Mrs. Wiley's chili beans and cinnamon rolls.

My favorite teacher was Ms. Wiggins, my PE teacher. Although I didn't play basketball, I admired how she drilled and prepared the girls' basketball team. She was a stern but fair teacher. My favorite subject was English. I enjoyed reading and writing poems, reading the literature stories that took you on an imaginary trip to another place in time, conjugating verb tense, and diagramming sentences. Professor Johnson was my principal when I started and ended my years of education at Carver High School. My school sports experience was that I served as one of the basketball statisticians. I enjoyed traveling with the teams and visiting other schools. It was my trip away from home! Another thing I would like to add is that teachers at Carver High School genuinely cared about the success of students in school and their lives beyond the school setting. There was mutual respect between the teachers and the students. My utmost advice for today's youth regarding education Is to establish good study habits, don't procrastinate, always maintain a good grade point average, finish high school, go to college, or find a trade that you are passionate about and know that "the sky is the limit". I earned my college degree at New Mexico State University. Finally, I would say choose your immediate friends wisely and your internet friends carefully!!

30. My name is **Michael A. Hanshaw**. I was Valedictorian of the Carver High School Class of 1970. I am the son of Mrs. Marguerite James Hanshaw and married to my classmate, Patricia Stallworth Hanshaw. During my school years at Carver, I studied Algebra I & II, Geometry, English I-3, History, Economics, Chemistry, Biology, Band, Choir, Physical Education, and Typing. I also took Drafting I & II at Pascagoula High School. Some of the things I remember most about my school years were:

a. Most of the classmates I graduated with in 1970 were my classmates in the first grade. During those 12 years, some classmates moved away, and new classmates joined the class. When I see the pictures of my classmates, there is usually a personal story attached to each one.

b. I will always cherish the camaraderie my class shared and the unity of the other classes of our day. We competed With one another in everything to make Carver High the best high school on the coast. That competition was always about trying to be better or do more than the other classes and never about tearing down or diminishing what they accomplished. At the end of the day, we were all Hornets.

c. most of my teachers lived in my community. They knew me and my family. They were not only my teachers, but they were also part of the village that raised me. I always wanted to do well in school, not only for myself but for my family and my teachers. I cared about what they thought of me because I held them in high esteem. They came to work every day, worked hard, and always showed that they cared. We were so fortunate to have such dedicated teachers who prepared us for life after high school, despite the many obstacles we all faced.

d. I remember being free to participate in as many activities as I wanted. I played in the band for four years and learned to play several different instruments. I sang in the choir for a couple of years. I played football during my last two years. I was a member of several clubs and served as Student Body President during my junior and senior years. My experience at Carver High greatly shaped the man I am today.

e. My favorite subjects were science and math. They came naturally to me and I loved the challenge of finding the answers. I never cared much for subjects that required me to remember dates and who said what. I liked most of my teachers, but if I had to pick a favorite, it would be Coach James McIntyre. He taught me geometry and algebra 2, was my running back and secondary coach in football, and I was his statistician for the basketball team. He always showed he cared about you, had great stories about college and military life, and inspired you to be your best.

f. Principal Willie Johnson was the Principal during my years at Carver. He provided great leadership and was always willing to listen to what you had to say. During my years as student body president, he always had my back and served as a mentor for me in leading the student government. With professor Johnson, we had someone who would stand up for Carver High. On the lighter side, whenever he would come on the school public address system, you did not want to be the reason for the announcement. Whether it was because your mom came to check you out of school or you were caught playing hooky, he would call you out, and everyone would have a good laugh at your expense.

Mrs. Marguerite J. Hanshaw, Class of 1938. We will miss you dearly.

g. I played football for two years and was on the baseball team. In the years leading up to playing, Coach Jones and/or Coach Knight would come by to ask my mom if I could play football. Her answer was always the same, NO. When she finally relented, I was a happy camper. It was an honor to play for the Hornets football team. I played running back and safety. We were Co- champions in my junior year. I was not much of a baseball player. It was still fun to be with the guys. I think I have said enough.

My advice to today's youth is to get an education for yourself. You and your children will be the main beneficiaries. You really can BE almost anything you want. Education is the key to unlocking what life has in store for you. You need an education whether you want to be a welder or a rocket scientist. The one person who has the most control over what you will do in life is you. If you want to own your own business or home, retire and live a comfortable life, and leave a legacy for your children, then get an education.

31. My name is **Betty Miller Mitchell** and I graduated from Carver High School in the Class of 1970. I took all courses required for graduation. My favorite courses were English and History. What I remember most about our school days was the closeness of students at Carver High School. In particular, I recall the pranks that boys would pull off. Such things would get on Mr. Ellis' nerves. As our homeroom teacher, he dubbed us the 'barbarians' because we were so hardheaded. He loved us anyway. My other favorite teachers were Mr. Richard Moore, Mr. James Winters, and Mr. Marvin Pickett. Mr. Johnson was our principal and did an effective job despite restrictions beyond his control.

I did not play sports or play in the high school band. I did sing in the choir under the direction of Mr. Richard Moore. Some of the happiest years of my life were at Carver High School. My support of alumni activities and the many friends I made in high school have lasted to the present time.

The History of Carver High School: 1890 – 1970 **103**

My advice to today's youth regarding education is that they should get as much education as possible. The world is continuously changing and education is absolutely essential to any plan to become successful in life. Getting a trade is a great option and so is going to college for two or four years. Get the education required under your belt to reach your goals and fulfill your dreams. I completed my nursing education by earning my Associate Degree and specializing in Medical Surgery Nursing. I hope all students will find their special area of interest as well.

32. My name is **Sandra Harris-Hooker**. I graduated in the Class of 1970. I took all classes required for graduation but I always had a love for the sciences (i.e., biology and chemistry). This eventually led to my earning a Ph.D. in Developmental Biology and completing a Postdoctoral Fellowship in Cardiovascular Pathology. In the photographs below, I was the

Keynote Speaker at Morehouse School of Medicine's 38th Fall Convocation & White Coat and Pinning Ceremony this year (2022). The institution will name a wing of a new Research Building in my honor.

One of my favorite teachers was Ms. Gibson basically because she was always so well "put together" and professional in her demeanor. With that said, Ms. Blake was an equal favorite for a different reason. I had and still have a special feeling for Ms. Blake because she was so 'down to earth' with a genuine heart for her students.

While sports were not a part of my school experience, I played in the band and the band traveled with the football team. I enjoyed the game as much as I enjoyed playing with the band during halftime. I knew the game well, so I was somewhat of a 'football junkie'.

There was one thing that was very memorable for me about my time at Carver, other than my meeting my soul mate and future husband. My dear friend Mike (Hanshaw) may recall this. That is, my class, the Class of 1970, was the last class to graduate from Carver High School. The school system wanted to close Carver as a high school and have us go over to Pascagoula High for our final year. We pushed back and threatened to have a 'sit-out' if not allowed to graduate from Carver. Although I understand that the school system could have demanded that Carver should close as a high school that year, I am so glad that we were able to graduate from Carver High School.

My advice to today's youth regarding education is to remember that education is <u>one</u> of the key accelerators to a successful life. I underscore <u>one </u>because there are several other keys including, but not limited to, knowledge, wisdom, determination, and most important, discernment. A high school or even a college education may potentially give you a good head but you need to have the heart to do the right thing with your educational endeavors. Nelson Mandela once said, "a good head and good heart are always a formidable combination".

33. My name is **Walter A. Hanshaw**. I attended Carver High School but completed my last two years at Pascagoula High School. I graduated in the Class of 1972. My wife is **Barbara Ellis Hanshaw**. She completes me. Barbara earned and was awarded a Hornet Blazer and the title **Honorary Hornet** some years ago for her support of the PN/CHS Alumni Association, Inc. I have submitted a picture of my participation in the PHS *Ebony Blanche Club*. I served as its President during part of my time at PHS (first row, black leather jacket). I had a large Afro **then**. As an Heir, I enjoyed placing our Hornet signs in the yard during reunions. I was especially happy that the Class of '72 won a trophy in 2019 for "*Respect Yourself*" [Staple Singers].

At CHS, I started taking all of the required courses for graduation. I remember most that everyone at Carver High was pulling in the same direction on behalf of our future. I went on to complete my higher education in Radio, Television, and Film at the University of Southern MS. I have worked as a DJ and had my radio talk show (The Sexy Sagittarian) on WTAM in Gulfport. I worked for over 40 years as a certified Senior Health Physics Technician and received awards for writing safety measures that benefited plant workers across the industry who, like me, performed their jobs in radioactive environments. I traveled by car from coast to coast and lots of points in between. I could not have done this without putting *education first* ... and having God in my life as my co-pilot.

I learned the value of this combination with the help of my mother, Mrs. Marguerite J. Hanshaw, and all of my older siblings: James, Corine, Larry Gene, and Michael. Larry Gene owes me because I talked him into working in the nuclear industry.

Afterward, we talked about our experiences in the industry all the time. He thanked me for convincing him to make the switch to greener pastures. His bills disappeared. My advice for today's youth is to understand that education is vital to your success in life. Study. Study. Study!!

34. My name is **Leonard James McEwen**. I attended Carver High School until 1970. My class was the second to graduate from Pascagoula High School due to integration. I would have preferred to graduate from Carver High School but the situation was out of my control.

Leonard James McEwen,
Heir, Class of 1972

The subjects I studied were math, history, and English. My favorite teacher in high school was Mr. McIntyre. History was my favorite subject. Mr. Johnson was my favorite principal. I did not play sports but I was in the band. I have included a photograph of my days at Skip Street Elementary and one from the 1940s of my mother, Mrs. Audrey C. McEwen. See her photo and others of me later in my statement.

The advice I have to offer is that it is vital to focus on getting your education so that you will be able to make the most of your future. I feel that young people should listen to the wisdom offered by elders, teachers, and others who are trying to help them. This same advice worked for me.

Some of my mother's schoolmates were: From L, front row: Iona Hyde, Grace Durden Hanshaw, and Norma Faye Harvey. **From L, back row**; Maria Graham Robinson, Professor H. L. Whisenton, V. P. Watts, and *Audrey Cook McEwen*. Professor Whisenton later went on to become principal at Magnolia High School in Moss Point and Mrs. Vivian P. Williams-Watts was a popular teacher at Carver High School.

CHAPTER 3

Shaping Our Legacy Going Forward

Chapter Three presents (1) archival information describing the tireless efforts of the **Constitution Committee and its leadership** that worked to complete the *constitution* of the PN/CHS Alumni Association (pre-and post-1985); (2) several **community pastors** whose *spiritual guidance* helped shape a moral center within the hearts of teachers and students at Carver High School. While there were certainly other religious leaders, three of them were honored by our Alumni Association for their contributions to Carver High School; (3) several *History Nuggets* that spotlight students and teachers for their unique contributions to the legacy of Carver High School; (4) former **CHS Hornets and Magnolia High School Monarchs** who participated in the 2022 *Smithsonian Voting Exhibit which sought to educate students across the Pas-Point community about the history and importance of voting;* (5) Archival class photographs of

Carver High School *graduation classes, reunion celebrations,* and a look at the *faces of The Heirs.* The Heirs are descendants *of PN/CHS Hornets. M*any of them are already actively supporting the PN/CHS Alumni Association, Inc., and will be counted on to lead it into the future; and (6) **What Hornets Have Become.** In this section of Chapter 3**,** a variety of career areas paint a *mosaic of achievements* by Hornets and Heirs. Supported by values taught at home, in church, and by academic roots anchored in our experiences at Carver High School, may Hornets and Heirs everywhere continue to shape our legacy going forward. Enjoy!!

Part 1:

Pascagoula Negro/Carver High School Alumni Association, Incorporated

Heart of the Hornets

The PN/CHS Alumni Association, Inc. is a Not-for-Profit Organization

Tucker Street view of the entrance to Carver High School

View of shop entrance at Carver High School

…food was always nourishing and served hot! Others may differ …

May 30, 1985 envelope containing correspondence from Jackie Elly and Dorothy R. Harvey to finalize the Writing of the PN/CHS Alumni Association's Constitution.

PN/CHS Alumni Association Officers
1995 - 1998

President . . . . Stanley Moore
[See arrow] Class of 1962

Vice President . . . . Dorothy Richardson Harvey
Class of 1963

Recording Secretary . . . . Lynette Fox Shackleford
Class of 1968

Corresponding Secretary . . . . Joyce Adams Shannon
Class of 1965

Treasurer . . . . Alfredia Colston
Class of 1968

Chaplain . . . . Rev. Langston Pickett
Class of 1958

Pascagoula Negro/Carver High School alumni members who are among those planning the 2009 reunion are, from left, front row, Catherine Huckleby, Linda Evans, Sharon Thompson, Peggy Kennard, Sandra Barnes; back row, Samuel Moore, John DeFlanders, Alfredia Colston, Stanley Moore, Jaffus Holloway and Elbert Wright.

May 8, 1985

Dear Alumni:

Since the Reunion very little has happened. Enclosed is a draft of our Constitution and we are presently making plans for the Blue and White

Ball.

We are asking you to read the Constitution, make whatever changes you deem necessary and return it to us by June 01, 1985. The Constitution Committee will take these changes under consideration when revising the Constitution. We will then forward a copy to you.

Please, do not forget that it is almost time for us to pay our Alumni Membership and ($5.00), the due date is July 01, 1985. We will return your receipt and membership card to you.

The Blue and White Ball will be June 29, 1985, at 9:00 p.m., at the Progressive Club on Convent Street, Pascagoula, MS. Advanced tickets will be $5.00 and $6.00 at the door. We will have live music. You may purchase your ticket at the Progressive Club. The dress code is semi- formal, the theme "Memories - The Way We Were". Tickets will go on sale Jima 08, 1985.

The local members showed little interest in the idea of having a court, so we have come up with another idea. We will still have a King and Queen but they will be selected on the night of the Ball by being the oldest alumni in good standing. We will make this determination from the infor- mation on the reverse side of the tickets. These two people will reign until the Ball next year, at which time we hope to select our King and Queen based on class competition.

Sincerely,

Dorothy Harvey
Dorothy Harvey

A. Jackie Elly
A. Jackie Elly

Co-Chairpersons

[985 Letter Regarding Alumni Constitution and other matters

Description of the PN/CHSAA, Inc.'s Constitution and Related Components

Constitution and Articles

President and Board Officers
Lay Board Member(s)

Board Activities

Omnibus Board
Member(s)

Examples of Board Activities

Alumni Association Scholarships

Draw Down
& Induction Ceremony

PN/CHS Wall of Fame*

Class Sponsored Scholarships

Alumni Ball

Alumni Parade of Classes

Pas-Point School Support

Disaster Response

PN/CHSAA, Inc. Association Dues

Obituary Response

Relationship to Wall
of Fame (WOF) Committee

Neighborhood Parade and Judging of Class Floats

Announcement of Parade Trophy Winners

Crowning of King and Queen

WOF Scholarship Award Ceremony

*Achievements and photographs of Wall of Fame Members can be viewed in the gymnasium of the Aaron Jones Family Interactive Learning Center.

Mission Statement
Message from the President: Andrew Jackie Elly, Class of 1967

Hornets and friends, it is my sincere privilege to welcome all of you to our 2019 biennial Reunion. It is most certainly an honor to have served as your President for the past eight years. We hope that your Reunion has been an enjoyable experience for Alumni, family members, and friends.

As we continue preparations, let us be mindful of those who paved the way for our successes. We can't say thanks enough to the teachers, our parents, and mentors for their leadership in molding us to be the role models they were to us.

This year is very heartwarming as my class "1967" celebrate our 52nd year of graduation. I thank all of them for cultivating lifelong friendships. All of us have become more of "brothers and sisters" rather than just classmates and schoolmates.

Being a HORNET is something special. When you return to your homes, remember we are "HORNETS FOREVER". Never allow anyone to shortchange this wonderful feeling and what it truly means. I shall always remember you in prayer as I ask you to remember me.

The PN/CHSAA, Inc. is a Not-For-Profit Organization

"Ain't No Stopping Us Now"

President Elly and other Hornets are at work making the reunion a group effort.

*L: Apostle Jeanette Kimble Martin, Rosie Bell Calhoun, Jackie Elly, Justine Montgomery
(Financial Secretary), and Dorothy Richardson Harvey (Lay Board Member)*

The PN/CHSAA extends its appreciation to the cities of *Pascagoula and Gautier* for their support which has enabled years of successful events defining our bi-annual reunion celebrations. We also recognize and thank the *Pascagoula Board of Education and its Superintendent* for their cooperation and support of PN/CHSAA activities. We especially applaud the School Board and Superintendent's decision to place our *Hornet image* on the renovated gymnasium floor within the Aaron Jones Family and Interactive Learning Center.

More Hornets Who Work to Make The Reunion Successful

In different years, Hornet alums prepare to celebrate another reunion. A prize is available if you are the first to correctly name the Hornets and reunion years on **this** *page and the* **next**.

PN/CARVER HIGH SCHOOL ALUMNI ASSOCIATION
2018-2019 OFFICERS

President: Andrew Jackie Elly `67

Vice President: Melba Richardson `72

Secretary: Linnette Fox Shackelford `68

Treasurer: Ruben Fountain `73

Financial Secretary: Justine Wright Montgomery `64

Sergeant at Arms: Samuel Moore `62

Chaplin: Apostle Jeanette Kimble Martin `68

Heirs Representative: Joe Davis

Immediate Past Alumni President: Sandra Burton Barnes `65

Lay Board Member: Dorothy Harvey `63

Hornets work and celebrate another Reunion

More Hornet History Nuggets (5-11)

Hornet History Nugget Number 5 (2007): Special to the Mississippi Press

Goode

Chapman

Martin

PASCAGOULA: Get set. Get ready. The Hornets are coming. The Pascagoula/Negro Carver High School Alumni Association is holding its reunion from June 29 through July 1 with the theme "Shining Stars." The reunion is held every three years and for the 2007 event, members from the Class of 1966 are the hosts. "This year's celebration will be a tribute to three stars of the community who, along with their church congregations, were instrumental in paving the paths for many students through their supportive efforts," said Ethel Crear of Moss Point, Class of 1966 treasurer. The three stars to be honored will be Rev. Leonard D. Chapman Sr., former pastor of Antioch Baptist Church; Rev. James T. Goode Sr., former pastor of Asbury AME Zion Church; and Rev. George J. Martin, former pastor of Union Baptist Church. While the three pastors are deceased, their families will be special guests at the reunion ball on June 30. They will be presented with plaques to honor each man.

Hornet History Nugget Number 6: Mrs. Pauline B. Young

The Pascagoula Negro/Carver High School Alumni Association, Inc. wishes to recognize the 30 years of service of Mrs. Pauline Brown Young who taught at Skip Street Elementary School under Principal Earnestine Fountain. Mrs. Young was mentioned by Jerry Blake and other former CHS students for her ability to motivate and teach students in ways that increased their understanding of every subject she taught. We honor and thank you for your service, Mrs. Young, on behalf of Hornets everywhere.

Hornet History Nugget Number 7:
Ms. Gerald Barnes ... Do What I Have Done

On one occasion at a recent alumni event, Ms. Barnes was asked to make a few comments. She did and then asked all students who were taught by her to stand. Of the crowd of over 400 people, only a few remained seated. This is a partial testimony to how many lives Ms. Barnes touched during her career as an elementary school teacher and principal, community college board member, Sunday School Superintendent, and community leader in the Pascagoula-Gautier area. All Hornets salute and thank you, Ms. Barnes, for all that you have given to Hornets and others throughout your life's journey.

Hornet History Nugget Number 8: Rev. L. G. Hawkins, Sr., Union Baptist Church; St. Peter and Sacred Heart Catholic Churches, and Alumni Glen T. Larkins and Burma Paris

The PN/CHSAA, Inc. wishes to recognize the *actions, support, and leadership of* (1) **Reverend L. G. Hawkins** (above) and the **Union Baptist Church Family** for their role in meeting various needs over the years across the state and in our local community. This was especially evident during Hurricane Katrina. For example, Mr. Marvin L. Pickett, Sr. and other members of the community were rescued because of actions taken by Rev. Hawkins and other members of Union Baptist who went door-to-door in a boat checking on church members; (2) **St. Peter** and **Sacred Heart Catholic Churches** for hosting numerous alumni social events and other programs vital to the success of the PN/CHSAA, Inc.; and (3) Alumni **Glenn T. Larkins and Burma Paris** for the number of people in Pascagoula they rescued during Hurricane Katrina.

Hornet History Nugget Number 9:
Mr. Melton Harris, Jr. Jackson County Supervisor, District 2

Best wishes and success to the PN/Carver High School Hornets on their 2019 Biannual Class Reunion Event

'Let the work which I have done speak for me'

No fewer words than those above can describe the honesty and tireless dedication of Supervisor Melton Harris, Jr. whom God has called to rest. The PN/CHSAA, Inc. and Jackson County are grateful for his service.

Hornet Nugget Number 10: Carver High School and Magnolia High School Alumni participate as panelists in The Smithsonian Institution's Voting Exhibit, Performing Arts Center, Pascagoula, MS, September 7, 2022.

The six panelists responded to questions about voting in Pascagoula and Moss Point and, along with other speakers, discussed additional views about voting statewide, especially along the MS Gulf Coast.

Smithsonian Program Moderator, Elizabeth Green poses questions to panelists

From L: Former MS Representative Billy Brumfield, retired teacher Gwen Beard, and Pharmacist Clarence Dubose, Magnolia High Alumni; Larry G. Hanshaw, Ph.D., Georgia P. Jones (CHS Poet Laureate), and former City Councilman and CHS teacher Marvin L. Pickett, Sr. are panelists representing Carver High School at the Smithsonian Exhibit program on voting.

Pat Davis, gives comments and greets the audience and panelists as a Committee Member with The Smithsonian Institution's Voting Exhibit, September 7, 2022

Mr. Mitch Ellerby, Program Speaker, *addresses the importance of voting at the Smithsonian Institution's Voting Exhibit Program, on September 7, 2022.*

Mr. Ellerby emphasized the power of voting and how it is the responsibility of all of us to be *registered voters* and **vote** to ensure that the changes wanted will help shape America into a country that reflects all of our needs. An often repeated takeaway by others regarding Mr. Ellerby's remarks was: 'if you don't vote, don't complain'. Get registered and VOTE!!

Smithsonian Voting Exhibit Panelists

*Magnolia High School graduate and former
State House Representative Billy Brumfield*

*Magnolia High School graduate and
former teacher Gwen Beard*

Magnolia High School graduate
Dr. Clarence Dubose

Panelist Gwen Beard (second from left) and Fellow Magnolia High
School Alumni Attend The Smithsonian Voting Exhibit Program

Magnolia High School Monarchs and Carver High School Hornets were **fierce competitors** during years of competition across the board of sponsored school activities. **We did not let this rivalry,** however, overshadow the joint support of and participation in The Smithsonian Voting Exhibit Program.

*Carver High School graduate, member of
the Archives Committee and PN/CHSAA
Poet Laureate Georgia P. Jones*

*Former CHS teacher and City Councilman
Mr. Marvin L. Pickett, Sr.*

Larry G. Hanshaw, Ph.D., Professor
Emeritus, University of MS

Every panelist above contributed important perspectives about voting during the Smithsonian Institution program. On behalf of all participants, and especially **Ms. Pat Davis**, a Committee Member of the Voting Exhibit Program, we extend our thanks to The Smithsonian Institution for the high educational value of the pictures, artifacts, and stories that detail the struggles and eventual victories embedded in past and ongoing efforts to achieve voting rights for all Americans.

Carver High School Hornets and guests show support for the Smithsonian Voting Exhibit
held on September 7, 2022, at the Performing Arts Center, Pascagoula, MS

I'll make you an offer you can't refuse: Win the prize associated with correctly naming every person in the above picture. Email or phone calls are accepted.

Hornet History Nugget Number 11

Heir Bernard A. James, Colonel, USAF (Ret.) shared a valuable artifact about voting in the Mississippi Delta (Itta Bena, MS) in 1955. The three-page artifact contained 21 questions to be answered in writing. It was passed on by his father PN/CHSAA, Inc. Wall of Famer John A. James (below).

Historical Artifact Describing the voting process during 1955, page 1

Very few Mississippians today have seen the two pages of the voter registration document presented here. A reading of the two pages makes it clear that the designers of this document intended to suppress voting using the ability to read and write fluently as its tools. Words or phrases such as "… your occupation", "by whom are you employed" or "reasonable interpretation" have little to do with being able to mark a circle or fill in a block appropriately to cast a ballot for the candidate of your choice. What if you have no job or your *interpretation* of a passage in the state constitution of Mississippi does not meet the personal interpretation of the person in charge? Such was the peril of voters, *particularly black voters*, in the MS Delta and across the state. It is also voter suppression to have a jar of *jellybeans* handy and require that one wishing to vote first state the *number of jellybeans* present in the jar. A jar of jellybeans was displayed and its presence was explained, along with other voting-related artifacts and pictures, in the excellent Smithsonian Voting Exhibit. The jar of jellybeans **was not there** as a "treat for kids" as one (white) teacher thought. This, however, is why the *civil rights era* and *voting* in America must be taught in schools.

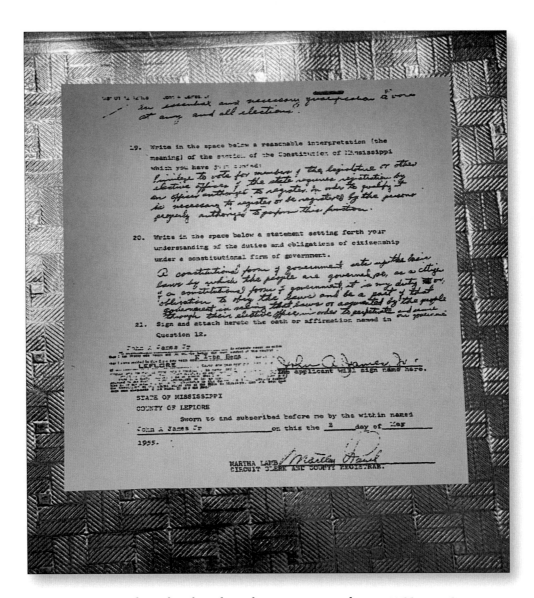

Historical Artifact describing the voting process during 1955, page 2

Part 2
The Wall of Fame (WOF) Committee

Message from Atty. Brenda Miller Johnson, First WOF Committee Chairperson, Class of 1968

In 2015, I became the first Wall of Fame (WOF) Committee Chairperson. My vision was to create a team of alumni members who would be known as the WOF Committee. The Committee would take whatever steps necessary to be the unconditional vessel of support for our PN/CHS Alumni Association. The committee's mission would be to provide scholarships to students accepted at a college or trade school of their choice. The WOF's ideas and financial contributions also might become an inspiration for those who would one day stand in our shoes as leaders and also give back. Hence, the team's guidelines and requirements would not provide scholarships based solely on scholastic scores but include family circumstances, heirship, community involvement, and social or financial standing as well. So long as the scholarship applicant is legitimately related to a PN/CHS alumni member or heir in good standing, the doors would be open to assist in their pursuit of a degree beyond high school.

Therefore, my vision dictated that somehow each qualified student would receive a WOF scholarship. Sharing this vision with other committee members expanded financial assistance not only to top-rated candidates but to others in need as well. Currently, three pools of scholarships have emerged: First place college, First place high school, and a third tier of financial assistance known as the TST (Toothpaste, Soap, and Travel) Scholarship. It is the third group that has met the expectations of my vision. Since 2015, all applicants have received scholarships at every tier. Although I served from 2015 to 2019, it is still a source of pride to see that my original vision now under new leadership continues to evolve and grow. The WOF Committee gives and students receive.

Message from Mr. Michael A. Hanshaw, MBA, WOF Committee Chairman (2019-present), Class of 1970.

The Wall of Fame Committee is a select group of Pascagoula Negro/Carver High School Alumni Association (PN/CHSAA) members who have distinguished themselves in their chosen careers. Members serve as role models and are dedicated to reaching back to help the next generation of Hornets achieve the career of their dreams. The Wall of Fame Committee supports the mission of the PN/CHSAA by providing scholarship awards to high school seniors and college students pursuing a college degree or a vocational skill. These scholarships aid in the development of vibrant citizens of our global society. Other officers of the WOF are Dr. Flora Randle Dees ('69), Secretary, Rev. Dr. Ann Pickett-Parker ('60), Chaplain, and Dr. Larry G. Hanshaw ('65), Treasurer.

The WOF Gold Medallion and PN/CHSAA Jacket and Accessories

Awarded to Inductees to the *PN/CHSAA, Inc.* ***Wall of Fame***, the **WOF Medallion,** along with the official Jacket of the Association and accessories, is worn by WOF members during official functions of the Association. The gold medallion bears the year of induction, the name of the inductee, and the Association's name. It symbolizes the distinguished accomplishments of a WOF member and the commitment to always "give back".

List of Wall of Fame Committee Officers: 2015 -2023

Atty. Brenda Miller Johnson, Committee Chairperson, Class of 1968: 2015 - 2019

Michael A. Hanshaw, MBA, Committee Chairman, Class of 1970: 2019 - Present (2023)

Dr. Flora Randall Dees, Secretary, Class of 1969: 2019 - Present (2023)

Rev. Dr. Ann Tyrus-Pickett Parker, Chaplain, Class of 1960: 2019 – Present (2023)

Larry G. Hanshaw, Ph.D., Treasurer, 2015 – Present (2023)

Introduction to Part 3

Hornets everywhere owe a debt of gratitude to the PN/CHSAA, Inc., its Archives Committee, all Reunion Year Classes, and our Heirs for documenting in words, artifacts, and photographs the celebration of our history as Carver High School Hornets. Efforts to expand what is presented here are ongoing. Artifacts of any kind shared with or given to the Archives Committee and your *periodic monetary* contributions will be greatly appreciated. You can help replace or restore what has been lost. Please contact: **PN/CHS Alumni Association, Inc., P. O. Box 1761, Pascagoula, MS 39568-1761.**

Part 3
Archival Class Photographs and Hornet Reunion Celebrations

1. Second and Third Grade Classes in 1941 likely became PN/CHS Graduates in 1950-1951

2. Class of 1945: Nadine McInnis Brown, Mildred Edwards Cook, Peter Martin, Potreen Martin (deceased), Ruth Kimball Barefield Pendleton, Margaret Thoms, Grace Hanshaw Travillion, Alma Williams, and Geneva Weary (deceased).

3. Class of 1948: 1stRow, L-R: Barbara Boudreaux, Isabelle McInnis, Lucille Boswell; 2nd Row, L-R: Bostic Cherry, Earnestine Cunningham, Rozena Jackson, Alma Williams, and James Newkirk.

4. Class of 1952, PNHS

5. *Class of 1953 (50th Anniversary) and Class of 1954 (49th Anniversary) Celebrate Reunions: First Row, L-R: Lottie Herger Ware, Lenora Barnes Reed, Clara Johnson Fluker, Ruth Barrett Burney, and June Harrison Slaughter; Second Row, L-R: Earnestine Price Sylvester ('54), Willie Williams ('54), Oliver Halthon ('53), Raife Pickett ('53), Sadie Whitehead Taylor ('53), B. B. Jennings, Jr. ('53; Third Row, L-R: Joe Louis Adams ('54), State Stallworth ('54), Lucille Brown Durden ('54); Helena Joyce Dubose ('53), Edward King ('53), and Alberta Martin Moore ('53).*

Special to The Pascagoula Press

6. Class of 1956: 1st Row, L-R: Vivian P. Williams (Class Sponsor), Jacqueline Patton, Willie Mae Ducksworth, Carrie Epps, Joyce Williams, Vernell Flowers, Nonnie Malone, and Mr. B. B. Jennings, Principal]. 2nd Row, L-R: William Ward, Eli Nelson, Johnny Williams, Bobby Pierce, J. B. Carter, Roger Mays, Emile Cook, and Claudette Richardson (not shown).

7. Class of 1955-56. Class Members are Edward Blake, Jerry Blake, Ben Brack, Annabelle Dennis, Don Jennings, Barbara Joyce, Roosevelt Lett, John Patterson, Rose Pears, Claudette Richardson, Geraldine Stewart, Bruce Williams, and 3 unidentified classmates.

8. Class of 1957. 1st Row, L-R: Unidentified, Don Elwood Jennings, Laura Harris, Ethel Anderson, Gloria Roberts, Gwendolyn Cobb, Nicholas Barnes, Annabelle Dennis, Edna Ruth Harris, Barbara Jones. 2nd Row, L-R: Lillie Mae Bohannon (Wright), Rose Peairs, Geraldine Stewart, Unidentified, Jerry Blake, John Patterson, Jerry Jefferson, Unidentified, Edwin Butler, Charles B. Barnes, Edward Blake, Roosevelt Lett, Fred Rogers, James D. Winters.

9. Class of 1958. James A. Hanshaw, M.Ed., (L) [USAF Veteran (Strategic Air Command Crew Chief) and former Social Studies teacher, Pascagoula-Gautier Schools. John D. Harrison, Jr., Class of 1958 (R), earned his master's degree in Educational Administration. Harrison is also a member of the 2017 PN/CHSAA Wall of Fame.

10. Class of 1959.

11. Class of 1960. 1st Row, L-R: Corine V. Hanshaw, Melloness Magee, Ann Tyrus, Valetta Thompson, Betty Joe Brown, Charles Fornett, Corine Thompson, Ida Mae Seals, Shirley B. Barnes, Ethel Norvel, Betty Roberts, Carrie Webster. 2nd Row, L-R: Robert Jennings (Archives Committee Chairman), Thelma Ruth Lamar, Jimmie Dale Jenkins, Dannie Mae James, Janice Harrison, Nellie Peairs Gary, Gladys Lyles, Espanolla Patterson, Nathaniel Coleman, Georgia P. Jones, Jessie Lee Thornton. 3rd Row, L-R: Rayford L. Salters, Archie L. Catchings, Juliarene Miller, Willie Poole, Robert Thompson, Lucille Pharr, Martin Henry, Estella Ducksworth, George Williams, Evelyn Hamilton, and Willo Dean Wilson.

12. Corine V. Hanshaw Chikeka, Ph.D., Class of 1960. First Oboe Player in the CHS Concert Band.

As a music teacher in Meridian, MS, her high school band performed on tours in five different states: MS, KY, MI, AL, and CA. Heir **Chinyere Chikeka**, PHS Class of 1991, read this information to me from her mother's vita.

13. Class of 1962. Commander Ellis Eugene Hodges, US Navy (Ret.), Master of Science in Public Administration, achieved Navy Medical Manager of the Year and several other awards. Commander Hodges is a 2017 PN/ CHSAA Wall of Fame member and an active member of the WOF Committee supporting scholarships for today's college students and high school graduates.

14. Calvin Huey, Ph.D., Class of 1963; Calvin and Debra Huey under his WOF Induction photo

First African American to star in football and he taught classes at the US Naval Academy. His photo and accomplishments are displayed there in Annapolis, Maryland.

15. Class of 1963. Sam Moore (R) and his nephew, S. Gordon Moore, during the 2015 Reunion.

Other Moore Family members hold awards given to WOFamer and former President, Stanley G. Moore, Class of **1963,** during the 2015 Reunion.

16. Class of 1963 members at the 2007 Reunion.

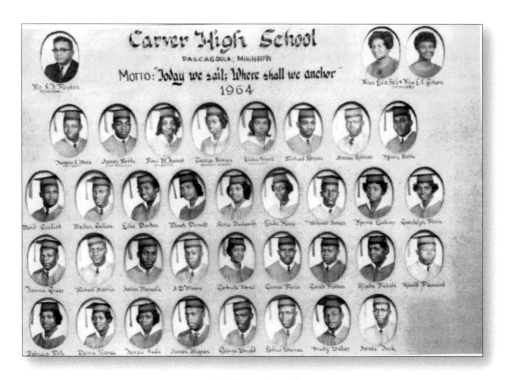

17. Class of 1964.
Principal: Mr. Payton and Sponsors: Ms. Lola Bell and Ms. Lou Ethel Gibson.

18. Class of 1965 Parade Float Entry, 2019 Reunion. Designer: Gill Autmon, Class of 1965.

Class of 1965 at the 2019 Reunion Ball.

Hornets celebrate another reunion.

Class of 1965 at the 2019 Reunion.

Look at the **italicized names** in the Class of '65 Roll. Can you correctly match the names with those in the photographs? **I'm on Facebook. Holler at me!**

Class of 1965's 2019 Reunion photo.

Class of 1965's 2nd Place Trophy: 2013 Reunion ['What I Say' by Ray Charles].

Class of 1965 Roll

Abrams, Walter Ernest III

Adams, Joyce Elaine

Autmon, Gill

Barial, Carolyn Novella

Booth, Dorothy Annel

Brown, Lugenius

Brown, Francis Evelyn

Brown, Wendell Wilkie

Burton, Sandra Anlee

Burton, Vonciel Odear

Colvin, Johnny Frank

Cook, Saundra Patricia

Cunningham, Carol Yvonne

Davis, Peggy Ann

Davis, Willie Lee

Duffy, Gerald Hawthorne

Evans, James Howard

Fisher, Roland Charles

* Hanshaw, Larry Gene

Harris, Beverly Ann

Harris, Mary Faye

*** Harris, William Lloyd

Hasty, Nanresa Angela

Henshaw, Beverly Ann

Jackson, Elliott

Jackson, Raymond

**** Johnson, Catherine Marie

Jones, Patricia Ann

Kimball, Tressie Mae

Lamar, Gloria Dean

Lett, Carolyn

**** Magee, Johnny Earl

Magee, Ora Lee

Mann, Willie Bell

McCreary, Betty Carolyn

McCullum, Patricia

Miskel, Robert Bailey

Murray, Annie Kate

Nichols, Alice Marie

Knowles, Emma Jean

Parker, Barbara Jean

Parker, Bobby Joe

*** Patton, Richard Marshall

Phillips, Dolores

Randall, Depriest

Roscoe, Elijah

Robinson, Raymond

Rogers, Clyde

Sabino, Carolyn

Sipp, Fred

Sipp, Leroy

Stallworth, Isaac

Stewart, Ora

Thomas, Samuel

Thompson, Robert

Walker, Ruth

** Wiley, ONeil

Woodson, Matthew

*Highest Honor

**Second Highest Honor

***Third Highest Honor

****Fourth Highest Honor

Class Sponsors:

-Mr. Aaron Jones

-Mr. James E. Taylor

19. Class of 1966. Class Officers.
Williene Coleman-Otis, President   Bobby Ward, Co-Treasurer
Hollis McArthur, Vice President   J.T. Good, Chaplain
Linda Martin Evans, Secretary   Earl Robinson, Co-Chaplain

Class of '66 at 40th Year Reunion in 2006.

Class of 1966 at 2009 Reunion … Reflections of Time.

20. Class of 1967. We are Hornets for Life.

Class of 1967 poses for a 50-Year Graduation photo.

Class of **1967** Roster.

Autmon, Marvin L.	Floyd, Dorothy L.	Hoye, Doretha	Norvel, Evelyn C.
Barnes, Bernard	Fornett, Linda L.	Hoye, R. C.	Page, Patricia A.
Barnes, Diane J.	Furniss, Charles	Joe, Louis A.	Perryman, Beatrice D.
Betts, Maggie L.	Gill, Bennie E.	Johnson, Andrea L.	Pleasant, Joseph A.
Booth, Alma Deloris	Goode, Mary E.	Johnson, William L.(Dec.)	Porter, Patricia A.
Burton, Chauncey E.	Graham, Annie M.(Dec.)	Keaton, Bernistein	Richardson, Morris P.
Campbell, Wendell L.	Hardy, Thomas D.(Dec.)	Larkins, Glenn Thomas	Richardson, Robert L.
Chapman, Ida Ruth	Harris, Julius A.	Laster Dorothy (Dec.)	Russell, Virginia L.
Cook, Trenell (Dec.)	Hayes, Willie L.	Lewis, Lafon	Seals, Carolyn
Daniels, Irma	Henry, Estella	Lewis, Williams (Dec.)	Stallworth, Irvin, Jr.
Dorsett, Stokes A.	Hicks, Annie R.	McCants, Arthur, III	Steel, James E.
Elly, Andrew J.	Holbert, Harry L.	McInnis, James E.	Stennis, Willie B.
Fisher, Ann P.	Holloway, Mary L.	Magee, Herman Paul (Dec.)	Thigpen, Charles

Fisher, James E.	Hopson, Willie	Massey, Evelyn L.	Thomas, John T.
Thompson, Eric D.	Torrey, James A.	Walker, Charles E. (Dec.)	Ward, Robert G.
Watson, Herman T.	Wells, Josh L. Jr.	Wells, Kenneth	Wiley, Benny, Jr.
Williams, Lenro A. (Dec.)	Williams, Shirley A. (Dec.)	Williams, Thomas E.	
Wonoley, Mary A. (Powell)		Woodson, Lee R.	Wright, Donald

Class Sponsors: Mrs. Thelma Lucas (Dec.), Mr. B. B. Jennings, and Mr. Richard Moore

21. Class of 1968.

Class Motto: Beyond Every New Day's Horizon Is A Gleam of Hope For A Brighter Future

Class Roll:

Austin, Earnest	Bradford, Caroline	Ducksworth, Keith	Furniss, Claudette	*Hurd, Gwendolyn
Barial, Paul	Brazzle, Sandra	Durden, Rodney	Gill, Bobby	**Hurd, Julia
Barnes, Alma	** Brown, Marilyn	Durden, Rose E.	Graves, Freddie C.	Hyde, Patricia
Barnes, Judy E.	Burt, Willie Hue	Edwings, Clara	**Hall, Michael	Jefferson, James

Barnes, Wanda B.

Beans, Annie

Black, Fuerella

Johnson, Gerald

Johnson, Richmond

Jones, Sarah

Kimble, Jeanette

Kitchens, Earnestine

Kitchens, Sarah N.

Knowles, Claudine

Larkins, Theresa

LaFargue, Francine

LeRoy, Madeline

Lett, Annie

Lett, Robert

Lindsey, Joe E.

Lott, Paulette

McCullum, Kercelia

Calhoun, James

** Colston, Alfredia

Cook, Janet

McGee, Ruth

McInnis, Daryl

Marsalis, Eddie

Miller, Brenda

Miller, James C.

Morris, Eddie

Morris, Kinnard

Nichols, Posey

**Page, Marilyn

Parson, Felicia

Patton, Sharon

Pickett, Frances

Pleasant, Reginald

Poole, Robert

Roberts, Lillie

Fisher, Clara

Floyd, E. C.

Fox, Linette

Randall, Charles

Rasco, Nelly

Richmond, J. C.

*Rodgers, Julia F.

Riley, William

Sabino, Lloyd

Sowell, Maryland

Stallworth, Eva

Stennis, Bernestine

Stennis, Carolyn

Stewart, Jerry

Thomas, Leonard

Titus, Paulette

Travillion, Ken

*Ward, Mary T.

Harris, Charles E.

Henry, Herman

Holloway, Jaffuss

Watson, Raymond

Wales, Lester

Wiley, William

Williams, Clarice

Williams, Paul

** Willis, Shirley

Winters, James

*Highest Honors

**High Honors

Class Sponsor: Mr. Billy Knight

Joe, Alex

Johnson, Della

Johnson, Leroy

Mr. Knight is 4th Row, 6th person.

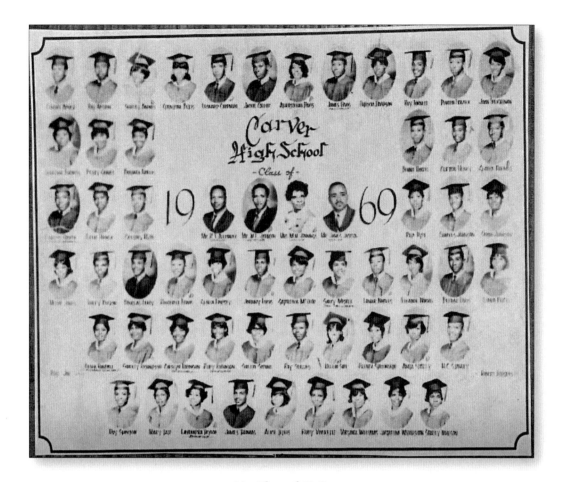

22. Class of 1969.

Class Roll:

Abney, Cemore M.	Frazier, Brenda Joyce	Hyde, Gregory	McLeod, Gaybrella Diane
***Abston, Ray Louis	Frazier, Devorn, Jr.	Hyde, Rita Maureen	Miller, Brenda Ann l
Barnes, Earl Lee	Freightman, Joan Katie	**Joe, Rose Antonia	*Miskel, Sallie Marie
Barnes, Shirley Diane	Furniss, Geraldine	Johnson, Charles	**Nobles, Lamar Venezuela
Betts, Geraldine	Graves, Betty Jo	Johnson, Sarah Mae	Norvell, Eleanor Louise
Chapman, Leonard	Harris, Barbara Mae	Keeton, Willey Jerome	Paris, Burma Randolph
Collier, Jackie	Harris, Bennie Eugene	LeRoy, Douglas Edward	Price, Linda Joyce
Davidson, Patricia Ann	***Clifton, Henry	Lewis, Roosevelt	**Randall, Flora Novella
Davis, Atherstean	***Holmes, George	*Lindsey, Gloria Ann	Richardson, Shirley
**Davis, James Terry	Hooker, Charles Everett	Lucas, Johnny Mack	Robinson, Carolyn LaFaye
Fornett, Roy Ecstine	Hooker, Lillie Murial	Manning, Glenn	**Robinson, Ruby Nayle

Class of 1969. First Place Parade Winners. King (Jaffus Halloway) and (Barbara Harris Skinner substituting for Queen (Dr. Flora Randall Dees).

Class of 1969 Roll (Continued)

Rodgers, Robert	Thomas, Earlie James
Sabino, Shelia Marie	Titus, Alice Faye
***Sellers, Roy Lee	Viverette, Ruby Jean
Sipp, Helen	Williams, Virginia Georgia
Stallworth, Brenda Delicia	Witherspoon, Jacqueline
Stanley, Hannibal Charles	Woodson, Shirley Ann
***Stanton, Roy	*Highest Honors
Tate, Mary Elizabeth	**High Honors
Taylor, Laurandra Marie	***Summer Graduation

23. THE MIGHTY CLASS OF 1970: Connecting with our Roots and enjoying the reunion.

From L-R, First Row: Patricia Ann Stallworth (Hanshaw), Peggy Kinard, Susie L. Larkins (Payton), Lela Stroud, Betty Miller (Mitchell), Barbara Lidell, and Geraldine Magee. L-R Second Row: Carl Burton, Larry Rodgers, and Charles Henshaw. L-R Third Row: Michael A. Hanshaw and Leroy Edwards.

Part 4

Episodes of Social and Economic Development

Before and after graduation from high school, many of us:

> Sold TV guides and Grit newspapers;
>
> Cut yards, sold scrap metal, and soda bottles;
>
> Became lifeguards, ticket-sellers at the local swimming pool and cleaned the "Rec";
>
> Washed windows at department stores;
>
> Loaded grain sacks in ships part-time;
>
> Worked part-time for local pharmacists, dentists, and optometrists (black and white);

Patronized (and some were employed by) businesses such as:

-The Shalamar	-VFWs along the coast
-The Blue Note	-The "Legion"
-Clubs at Keesler Air Force Base	-Joe McArthur's
-Sugar's	-The Progressive Club
-Mable's	-High Chaparral
-Miller's Teen Center and the Village Drugstore	-Kick-Off Club

… and the list goes on.

Most of our parents did not have funds for "allowances". We worked and played and always wanted to look good after a trip to one of the local barber shops (Mr. Brown, Mr. Budreaux, Skillet, or Mr. Harris or Mrs. Betts' Beauty Shop). Or, we got things cut or curled with a little *Royal Crown* at home. Some were even babysitters on the weekend. What a time!!

Part 5

Age of the Heirs: Continuation of a Legacy

The name "Heirs" defines relatives of those who attended or graduated from Carver High School. Heirs voluntarily work to support the mission, programs, and other activities of the PN/CHSAA, Inc. These **Hornets** recognize that the success they help to build now will lead to an even greater future for the PN/CHSAA. Many are graduates of and/or completed their final high school years at Pascagoula High School after 1970. They are forever bound to the history of our common roots which have, in turn, helped all of us achieve what we have become. One might recognize many of the Heirs shown in the next photograph. Mr. **Joe Davis**, front row (R) kneeling and wearing a tuxedo, is the current Heirs Committee Chairman.

Hornet Heirs

"Keeping It Going For The Future"

The Class of 1973 Hornet Heirs: Celebrating 45 Years.

President: Brenda Henry Terrell

Vice President: Walterene Norvell Gladney

Secretary: Yutaska Dailey-Sellers

Asst. Secretary: Cyrill Laster

Treasurer: Diane Capels Dees

Part 6

What Hornets and Heirs Have Become

Listed below are *examples* of careers **Hornets** have achieved before and after Carver High School was built in 1952. Such accomplishments are evidence of what can happen when you *try and never give up*.

- Medical doctors and nurses; including licensed pediatric practical nurses.

- Teachers K-12 and higher education professors; hospital employees

- Shipbuilding employees and management personnel; welder; tugboat engineers; recording artist/soul singer

- Lawyers; judges; tax preparers; city councilmen; ship painters; air condition installers and repairmen; self-employed carpenters

- Supervisors: Many are "Firsts" in their service to various local businesses and state agencies; draftsmen; wing of a medical school named to honor a Hornet's achievements

- Hornets and Heirs (continued)

- Professional football player; Super Bowl Winner; Decorated military servicemen

- High school, college, and graduate school degree holders; many others with trade-related certifications; high school football, track, and baseball coaches

- Medical research scientists at major universities; some are also Academic Deans and Emeritus Professors; Social workers (city, county, and state)

- Community College Board Appointees; some with service on the MS Institutions of Higher Learning Board; K-12 special educators and K-12 department chairs

- Poll workers; published book authors; military jet fighter pilots, and commercial airline pilots; military pilots; major leadership roles in churches across various faiths

- K-12 principals; former major oil company employees and air traffic controllers

- Major leadership roles in sororities and fraternities; city and state government supervisors; Health physics technicians and radiochemists at nuclear power plants

- Office secretaries at a major shipbuilding corporation; Community college instructors

- NOAA (National Oceanic and Atmospheric Administration) scientist; self-employed business owners; ministers, church deacons, and church business managers/treasurers

- City of Pascagoula employees and supervisors; professional musicians/singers, including an opera singer.

PN/CHS Heirs:

- Anesthesiologists; research scientist/international group leader at a major chemical company; self-owned business consulting manager

- Civil engineering project manager; college professors; Attorney-at-Law

- Surgical nurses; Sports medicine professional; Songwriter/Performer/Instrumentalist

- Retired military personnel; college professors; medical doctors.

Closing Thoughts

The History of Carver High School: From the Colored School to Carver High School captures many of the unique experiences and achievements of Carver High School Hornets and their heirs. The historical dedication of teachers, administrators, and religious leaders featured in this book is a testimony to what can happen when a community of leaders works together to provide all children opportunities for success in life despite the lasting challenges of America's racial divide. We could not have come to where we are without our parents who gave us life, love, and guidance along the way. This history book will hopefully be a lasting source of inspiration for all who seek a pathway to the acceptable fulfillment of their dreams.

Many things power and sustain us as we make our way through life. May the symbolism from a favorite poem enrich the aspirations of readers, Hornets, and Heirs everywhere:

I'M TIRED OF SAILING MY LITTLE SHIP CLOSE INSIDE THE HARBOR BAR.

I WANT TO GO OUT, FAR OUT TO SEA WHERE THE GREAT SHIPS ARE.

AND IF MY FRAIL CRAFT PROVES TOO SLIGHT

FOR THE WINDS THAT SWEEP THOSE BILLOWS 'ORE,

I'D RATHER GO DOWN IN A STIRRING FIGHT

THAN DROWN TO DEATH ON A SHELTERED SHORE.

—Unknown Author

Appendix 1

PN/CHSAA, Inc. Wall of Famers (T=teacher; C=Coach; P=Principal; Red=Deceased)

Name	Class Year	WOF Class	Name	Class Year	WOF Class
Ball, Marilyn Massey	66	4	Hooker, Sandra Harris	70	1
Bennett, Margie Joseph	66	4	Huey, Calvin	61	1
Bolton, Lou Ethel Gibson	T	4	Jackson, Elliott	65	3
Byrd, Mazie Parker	55	4	James, John A., Jr.	40*	3
Carter, J. B.	56	1	Jennings B. B., Jr.	T/53	2
Chikeka, Corine Hanshaw	60	2	Jennings, B.B., Sr.	P	1
Cobb, William	44	3	Jennings, Mattie Woods	T	1
Cole, Edwin	T	4	Johnson, Brenda Miller	68	2
Crear, Ethel Pharr	71	2	Johnson, Willie	P	1
Davis, J. Terry	66	2	Jones, Aaron	T/C	1
Dees, Flora Randall	69	1	Knight, Billy	T/C	1
Denning, Joe Ann Marsalis	66	3	Larkins, Glen	67	2
Duffy, Gerald	65	3	Magee, Herman	67	1
Elly, Andrew Jackie	67	3	Marsalis, James	64	1
Fisher, Roland	65	3	Martin, Lionel	64	1
Halton, Oliver	52	2	Mays, Nebraska	59	1
Hanshaw, Larry	65	1	McArthur, Hollis	66	2
Hanshaw, Michael	70	1	McEwen, Albert D., Jr.	70	2
Hardy, Thomas	67	1	McIntyre, James	T	4
Harrison, John, Jr.	58	3	Mitchell, Betty Miller	70	3
Harvey, Dorothy Richardson	63	2	Miller, Frank	65	2
Hodges, Ellis	62	3	Miller, George	59	1
Holloway, Jaffus	69	4	Moore, Alberta Martin	52	2
Holmes, Julia Rodgers	68	4	Moore, Richard	T	2

Appendix 1 (Continued; Note: * = 12 grades unavailable; others completed in 1940).

Class Name	WOF Year	Class Class	Class Name	WOF Year	Class Class
Moore, Stanley G.	62	1	Wright, Donald	67	4
Morant, Eula Randall	63	4			
Norvel, Paul	62	1			
Norvel, Robert	58	4			
Omobien, Linda Randall	70	2			
Parker, Ann Pickett	60	1			
Patton, Howard	52	3			
Pickett, Marvin L., Sr.	T/54	1			
Rainey, Barbara Joyce	57	3			
Randall, Booker T.	66	3			
Reed, Lenora Barnes	T/53	3			
Richardson, Morris	67	2			
Riley, Dinah Dorsett	64	4			
Stallworth, State, Sr.	54	1			
Stroud, Lela Lott	70	3			
Stroman, Lou Ann Pickett	66	4			
Taylor, James E.	T	3			
Thompson, Sharon Brown	66	3			
Waters, Terrell	54	2			
Watts, Vivian P. Williams	T/44	1			
Wells, Josh	67	2			
Wesley, Shirley Woodson	69	3			
Wiley, O'Neil	65	4			
Williams, Earnest	54	4			

Appendix 2

Founders and List of PN/CHSAA, Inc. Presidents

Dinah Dorsett-Riley, Class of 1964, Co-Founder and Secretary, PN/CHSAA, Inc., and **2019 WOF Member.**

PN/CHSAA, Inc. Presidents:

1. Pernell Huey (1987-1991)

2. Stanley G. Moore (1997-2001)

3. Elbert Wright (2005-2007)

4. Sharon Brown Thompson (2007-2011)

5. Sandra Burton Barnes (2011-2013)

6. Jaffus Holloway (2013-2015)

7. Andrew Jackie Elly (Co-Founder) and President (2015-2023)

Appendix 3

Dear Ole Carver High

Front   (1)

Rear   (2)

PN/CHSAA, Inc. Wall of Famer Glenn Larkins ('67)
points to cherished information about the HIVE   (3)

Black History Month T-Shirt: "Honoring the Ones That Paved the Way"

*Presented at the Black History Month program sponsored
by Pascagoula High School, February 2023.   (4)*

History Book Project Interview Questions

1. Please tell me your name.

2. During your school years, what subjects did you study?

3. What are some things you remember most about your school years?

   - Did you have a favorite teacher, subject, or principal?

   - Were sports part of your school experience?

4. Anything else you would like to add or talk about?

5. Do you have any advice for today's youth regarding education?

(5)

Market Street View, Pascagoula, MS

(6)

View of Plaza Seating for **Hornet Alumni Flame** *(sits on the orange base beneath the table). The* **Flame** *was dedicated during the 2019 Reunion celebration and is lit during the reunion.*

(7)

Inaugural Panther-Gator Challenge Game Honoring Carver High School for Black History Month; Pascagoula High School and Gautier High School, February 2023.

(8)

CHS Hornets enjoy the Panther-Gator Challenge game during Black History Month.

(9)

Attendees at the Panther-Gator Challenge game enjoy the action.

(10)

References

Black History Month News Segment. Television news coverage and description of the program presented by Pascagoula High School (See Appendix 3). Video not included in this book but is available from https://www.wlox.com/202302/01/carver-high-school-alumni-recognized-black-history--celebration/

- Pritchett, C./MS Press (June 22, 2004). Reunion photo of Carver High School Hornets [seated on school steps], P.1C). Pascagoula, MS: MS Press.

- Higginbotham, J. (1967). Pascagoula: Singing river city. Pascagoula, MS: Gill Press.

- Smithsonian Institution's Voting Exhibit Program (September 7, 2022). Photographs (13 in

- Hornet Nugget Number 10) used by permission of Pat Davis, Program Committee Member, and

- Smithsonian Voting Exhibit staff (See also related credits in (1) Acknowledgements and (2)

- Appendix 3: Dear Ole Carver High).

Index

The Index in this book arranges selected topics in alphabetical order. It is intended as a helpful guide to the book's contents.

W

Made in the USA
Columbia, SC
06 May 2023

3b8eb176-b123-4d19-b98d-d2ccad2e707cR02